THE JOY OF
Herbs

A Guide to Growing, Cooking, and Decorating

Contributing Writer ~ Carol Landa Christenson
Consultant ~ Kathi Keville
Projects Coordinator ~ Dan Newcomb

Publications International, Ltd.

Photo credits:
Front and back cover: ***Sam Griffith Studios.***

American Lamb Council; Ron Anderson/Midwestock; Cathy Wilkinson Barash; Burke/Triolo; Walter Chandoha; Catriona Tudor Erler; James Walsh Erler; Steven Foster;
FPG International: Robert Cundy; Art Montes De Oca; Mark Greenberg; David McGlynn; Victor Scocozza; Elizabeth Simpson; Thayer Syme; ***Sam Griffith Studios; International Olive Oil Council; Kathi Keville; Elvin McDonald; Kevin McGowan Photography; Jerry Pavia; Joanne Pavia; Photo/Nats; Positive Images:*** Patricia J. Bruno; Harry Haralambou; Jerry Howard; ***Sacco Photography; Silver Lining Graphics; Kevin Smith; Tom Tracy Photography; Lee Anne White.***

Illustrations: Mike Muir; Roberta L. Simonds.

Contributing Writer: Carol Landa Christensen

Consultant: Kathi Keville

Projects Coordinator: Don Newcomb
Contributing Project Designer: Maria Buscemi

Model: Pamela Kaplanes/Royal Model Management

Special thanks to Maureen Buehrli of The Herbal Connection and to David Merrill at *The Herb Companion* magazine.

Carol Landa Christensen has been a feature writer for the Springfield (Massachusetts) newspapers and has contributed to various magazines, including *Plants Alive* and *Gurney's Gardening News.*

Kathi Keville is the author of *American Country Living: Herbs* and *An Illustrated Encyclopedia of Herbs,* and the editor of the *American Herb Association's Quarterly Newsletter.* She has also written approximately 100 articles on herbs for national magazines.

Contents

Introduction

Herbs are probably the most popular and intriguing group of plants in existence. Over the centuries herbs have been used to flavor our foods, perfume our homes and bodies, decorate our gardens, and cure our ills. Herbs possess a natural grace and an alluring beauty that have made them hallmarks of culinary, decorative, and gardening simplicity. In the Eastern world, well before the Christian era, many books on herbal remedies were produced and, of these, some are still valued as authoritative.

Delicate in foliage, an herb garden complements any landscape.

Later, the pre-Christian Greeks and Romans cultivated herbs for medicinal use as well. Hippocrates, the father of medicine, used several herbs for their curative powers and taught his students these techniques. Herbs were even grown in monasteries all over Europe for medicinal and spiritual use.

With the development of more effective horticultural techniques, the popularity and use of herbs grew. By the early eighteenth century, herb gardens were common sights all over Europe and some colonists in New England were reported to have brought herbs along with them as reminders of the lush herb gardens of Europe.

As the Industrial Revolution brought advances in methods of agricultural prodution, many people moved from rural to urban areas. Herbs gradually lost their spiritual and medicinal mystique as science and its applications gained favor with an ever-expanding and city-dwelling populace. Urban dwellers, faced with limited accessibility to gardens and gardening, fell away from traditional attitudes toward herbs.

Herbs and their many functions were never eliminated from popular usage, however. In recent years,

Brilliant purple hues of anise provide a striking focal point in this colorful garden.

many people have grown more aware of the benefits and charms of these amazing plants. Herb gardening is now a full-time occupation for some, and a full-time hobby for even more. Herb usage is as varied and intriguing as the breadth of their scents and foliage.

What exactly is an herb? Because of their diversity, no group of plants is more difficult to define. A general rule is that an herb is a seed-producing plant that dies down at the end of the growing season and is noted for aromatic and/or medicinal qualities. Then how have we decided which plants to include in this book? We simply chose those herbs that we judge to be the most foolproof to grow and the most useful for cooking, potpourris, basic herbal cosmetics, and fresh and dried decorations for a beginning herb enthusiast.

Sooner or later, most of us decide to try our hand at growing a few of our favorite herbs. The effort may be a single basil plant in a small terra cotta pot or a small window box with parsley, oregano, or thyme. Once started, though, many gardeners find them-

selves increasing the number of herbs they cultivate simply because so many of them

Herbs are a centuries-old source for medicines, cosmetics, and culinary ingredients.

flourish with very little care. That terra-cotta pot becomes a 20 square foot garden and that window box springboards into a lush landscaped collection of fennel, garlic chives, and southernwood.

These rugged, hardy plants survive, and even thrive, in poor soil and wide temperature fluctuations that would prove too difficult for many other cultivated plant varieties. This same vigor makes herbs an admirable

Oregano (foreground) comes in many varieties, each with subtle differences.

choice for use in window boxes and other container situations where they're likely to be subjected to heat and dryness. A large part of their appeal is their natural ability to respond well to their surroundings without excessive soil preparation and rigorous care.

This book provides the basics on how to grow, propagate, harvest, and store the most popular herbs. It also includes ways on how to use them in your home and garden. Lists of herbs suited for certain uses such as potted plants, potpourri ingredients, and fresh arrangements are handy for quick reference. The encyclopedia section features a photo of each herb along with notes on its culture, hardiness, harvest and storage techniques, and uses.

Culinary enthusiasts will find an herb garden a tremendous opportunity for experimenting with traditional recipes. The seemingly inconsequential addition of just a teaspoon or two of a particular herb to an ordinary recipe can yield surprisingly flavorful results. Better yet, when attempting a recipe that calls for herbs, you'll have what you need on hand, fresh, and with no fear of chemical additives. A detailed chart lists a variety of food categories and corresponding herbs whose flavors best complement the flavors of specific dishes. Also included are several recipes for soups, sauces, breads, entrees, and marinades that make use of commonly grown herbs.

Herbs fit beautifully into any landscape. Ground-hugging thyme is a perfect choice for planting between the rocks in a flagstone walk. Tall clumps of angelica or rue provide attractive, dramatic accents in flower borders. Nasturtiums, calendulas, chives, and lavender all add vibrant floral color to a garden as well as attractive cut flowers suitable for decorative uses inside your home.

Whether you want to grow a few herbs in your kitchen window as a source of fresh flavoring for your meals, or you wish to design and plant an elaborate formal herb garden, the basic information you'll need to get started is provided here. As you become more familiar with herbs, you'll probably find yourself gradually increasing both the amount and the varieties you grow and *The Joy of Herbs* will help you along the way.

Due to their ease of cultivation and striking beauty, herbs are becoming popular additions to many gardens.

Growing Your Own Herbs

Growing your own herbs assures a fresh supply each year. In addition, you know exactly what you're getting. There's no need for concern that any unwanted chemicals have been added—a matter of particular importance with culinary herbs. Growing your own herbs also provides more aesthetic advantages. What could be more pleasant than the fragrance released by brushing past lush foliage as you wander through your garden? Although you can certainly enjoy many of the pleasures afforded by herbs without growing them yourself, there is always an added measure of enjoyment when they're the product of your own effort.

The numerous varieties of popularly grown herbs ensure finding a new favorite.

This chapter will show you how to grow herbs from seed, cuttings, potted plants, division, and layering. It also provides information on basic requirements for healthy plant growth. Our chart will help you identify those plants best suited to your site characteristics. It also notes whether plants are annuals (live one growing season), biennials (live two growing seasons), or perennials (may live up to 12 years), and how large you can expect each herb to grow when mature. Especially attractive landscape varieties are also noted. The soil and light section recommends ways to adjust your available conditions to better suit plants you may especially want to accommodate.

Many herbs will succeed under a variety of growing conditions. You may even find yourself with more herbs than you can use. When you look at that tiny seedling or rooted cutting, it can be very difficult to believe that all you'll probably need to keep fully supplied is one or two plants each of thyme, sage, rosemary, basil, parsley, mint, chives, tarragon, oregano, and marjoram. You'll probably need more plants if you cook large amounts of special ethnic foods daily that all use the same herbs, or if you plan to use large quantities of herbs for the herbal

Herbs are brightly colored and richly textured, so you'll find one for every purpose.

Most herbs thrive as potted plants whether overwintering indoors or grown as permanent fixtures for a terrace or window ledge.

vinegar, oil, bath, or wreath projects mentioned in this book. You will also want more plants for special landscaping designs.

If you find you've underestimated, add more plants. If you have an oversupply, herbs, whether growing plants or herbal products, are always welcome gifts. Most people are intrigued by herbs and enthusiastic about giving

them a try. Sharing your produce and knowledge with others is yet another enjoyable aspect of growing and preserving herbs.

SOIL AND LIGHT

Soil, light, and water are the three essentials for plant growth. While some plant species are very specific in their requirements, others are wonderfully versatile. They'll grow almost anywhere.

Fortunately, many of the most popular herbs fall into the latter category. The key to success with herbs is to select those that prefer the quality of soil and the amount of water and light you have available. For example, if you have an area of rich, moist soil with sun only part of the day, that's the ideal location for rue, sweet woodruff, peppermint, and spearmint. Many herbs such as sage, thyme, chamomile, and oregano survive in bright sun and dry, rocky or sandy soil that is fairly low in nutrients. As a result, it's relatively easy to grow these herbs successfully in many parts of the country without the rich garden loam and high water availability that ornamental garden plants frequently require.

Of course, it's also possible to manipulate soil, water, and nutrients to accommodate a specific plant's preference. If you don't have the right conditions to support a particular herb, you don't

Daisylike chamomile makes a colorful and aromatic addition to any garden.

have to do without. The best approach in most instances is to grow them in containers. Single plants can be grown in standard pots; several can be planted together in window boxes, half-barrels, or very large pots. Multiple plantings can be made up of one variety or a group of different varieties. Just be sure to combine those species that like the same soil, water, and light conditions in any one container.

To provide special soil conditions for a large number of herbs, fill an entire planting bed with the desired soil mix after removing the existing soil to a depth of 8 to 10 inches and choose herbs that do not produce deep tap roots. Another alternative is to construct a raised bed of the same depth. This latter choice works well where better drainage is needed or where more height will allow better plant visibility. Natural soil such as compost, lime, sand, or peat moss can also be added to the existing soil.

The three basic soil mix recipes listed on the following page will work well for most plant needs. Keep in mind that these are not rigid proportions. Unlike

STARTING YOUR OWN PLANTS

These herbs are especially receptive to cultivation from seed:

Basil

Calendula

Caraway

Chamomile

Chervil

Dill

Nasturtium

Summer Savory

cooking recipes, they can be varied somewhat without dire results.

Even though light conditions are more difficult to manipulate, they can be artificially adjusted to some extent. For example, if an area is too hot

and sun-filled, consider ways in which some shade can be provided. A fence or an arbor could be a quick shade source as well as an attractive permanent garden feature. Even simpler would be a planting of annual or perennial vines on a wooden or wire support. For a long-term shade source, consider planting shade trees and hedges.

When the problem is one of not enough light, the solutions are either to remove some of the shade by thinning existing trees and shrubs or to regularly shuttle plants in and out of the shaded area. To do this successfully, potted plants need to spend at least half of their days in a sunny location. Therefore, they should be of a small enough size or set on wheels to ease their transfer.

Another way to supply additional light, especially for herbs grown indoors, is with the addition of artificial light.

SOIL MIX RECIPES

SANDY, WELL-DRAINED MIX:

2 parts medium to coarse sand*

1 part perlite

1 part potting soil or garden loam

AVERAGE SOIL MIX:

1 part potting soil or garden loam

1 part moistened peat moss* or compost

1 part sand* or perlite

RICH, MOIST MIX:

1 part potting soil or garden loam

1 part moistened peat moss* or compost

NOTE: Do not use ocean beach sand because of the salt it contains. Get sand from a sand pit or builder's supply store.

Also, peat moss is acid, so avoid large amounts when growing alkaline-loving plants (this information is noted, when applicable, in the herb encyclopedia section).

Many herbs, such as these chives, will grow in a wide variety of soil conditions.

Lengthen the sunlight hours or strengthen the existing light by placing grow lamps over the plants. Grow lamps are available at many garden supply stores.

STARTING YOUR OWN PLANTS

There are five different ways in which new plants come into being. The simplest and least expensive source is from seeds. This is the best way to propagate most annuals and perennials. Among the herbs on our list (see page 23), those most easily grown from seed are basil, calendula, nasturtium, chervil, chamomile, summer savory, caraway, and dill.

A second easy and inexpensive source is by division. You physically pull apart the roots of a large perennial plant to create several smaller ones. Beginners should try to choose plants that have roots that sprout from the base and have more than one stalk. Simply pull a root clump from the plant and repot it. Among the herbs noted in this book that readily divide are thyme, spearmint, peppermint, chives, lemon balm, and sweet woodruff.

A third, more expensive plant source is purchasing potted plants from a nursery or garden shop. When there are no budgetary limitations, this is the quickest and easiest way to obtain an established herb planting. Of course, it's the only solution when no other source is available. Unless you have a friend who will share, it may be necessary to initially purchase at least one plant of rosemary, oregano, lavender, and specialty varieties of thyme, such as lemon and silver thyme. The same is true of certain unique flavors of mint. Many scented geraniums, tarragon, and horseradish do not produce seeds at all and must be either purchased or divided. Most annuals such as basil, borage, calendula, chervil, and dill are grown from seed or purchased.

The fourth source of new plants is through the taking and rooting of cuttings from perennials. To execute this method, segments of plant stems that will generate their own roots when cut from the parent are inserted into a growing mixture. Of the herbs listed in this book, those best propagated by cuttings are rosemary, lavender, and tarragon.

A fifth method is layering. Most perennial herbs with sprawling stems will work. Gently bend the stem without

GARDENING WITH RAISED BEDS

Raised beds are a good choice where soil is either of poor quality or nonexistent. Constructed of pressure-treated wood, reinforced concrete, or mortared brick, stone, or blocks, these beds can be of any length, but should have a soil depth of at least 6 inches. For easy maintenance, beds should be no wider than 4 feet. By filling some beds with a rich loam mixture and others with a more sandy, well-drained mix, it's possible to provide the ideal soil requirements for a wide range of plants.

WHAT TO LOOK FOR IN CONTAINER-GROWN PLANTS

Look for these signals when selecting plants grown in containers. They'll go a long way toward indicating how long the plant has been in the container and how it's been cared for during that time. Strong, vital plants that have been given good care have a far better chance of surviving when transplanted into the garden.

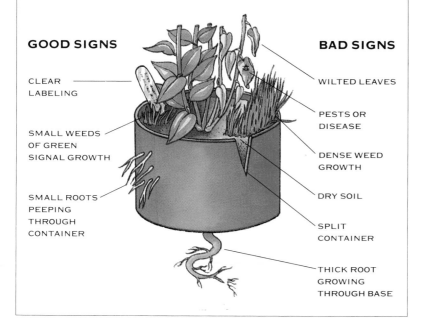

GOOD SIGNS

CLEAR LABELING

SMALL WEEDS OF GREEN SIGNAL GROWTH

SMALL ROOTS PEEPING THROUGH CONTAINER

BAD SIGNS

WILTED LEAVES

PESTS OR DISEASE

DENSE WEED GROWTH

DRY SOIL

SPLIT CONTAINER

THICK ROOT GROWING THROUGH BASE

removing it from the plant so that it touches the ground. Mound dirt over the stem, press the soil down, and keep it watered. When a root has formed, cut the stem from the mother plant. It can then be replanted. Allow a few weeks for this method to produce a viable new plant, and be sure to take special care of the original stem and the delicate new root structure of the new plant. Hyssop, lavender, oregano, and rosemary are all easily propagated by layering.

EQUIPMENT FOR STARTING PLANTS INDOORS

1. A fluorescent light fixture with full-spectrum grow lamp bulbs. Ideally, you should be able to easily raise and lower the fixture in order to maintain about 3 inches between the light bulbs and the plant tops at all times.

2. An automatic timer to turn the light fixture on and off each day is optional. However, it does take the worry out of trying to remember this twice-a-day chore. Since plants require between 16 to 18 hours of light daily, don't leave the lights on all of the time; darkness is also essential.

3. White or silver-colored reflectors placed around three, or all four, sides will bounce light onto plants from all angles. It will help keep them from leaning and stretching toward a single light source. A homemade reflector can be made of cardboard covered with aluminum foil.

4. If starting seed in a cool room, a thermostatically controlled heating cable should be laid under the seed boxes and pots. Bottom heat is more important than air temperature for growth.

5. A drip tray allows watering of seedlings from the bottom. Water poured into the tray is absorbed upward into the soil.

With enough light and proper attention, herbs grown indoors will thrive just as those grown outdoors.

STARTING FROM SEED

Seeds can be handled in one of two ways. They can be planted directly in the garden bed or vegetable row once the soil begins to warm; or they can be started in containers indoors and then transplanted to their final growing sites.

Those herbs best seeded in their permanent locations from the beginning include anise, borage, dill, caraway, summer savory, angelica, chervil, and coriander. These varieties don't survive transplanting well, and they don't like to have their roots disturbed. Many other herbs, such as nasturtiums, basil, calendula, parsley, chives, chamomile, and lovage grow so quickly and easily from seed that they can be planted in place.

STARTING FROM SEED

1. Once the soil is warm, cultivate and rake the bed to loosen and break up any existing lumps. Smooth the area.

2. Plant the seeds three to a cluster, 3 to 6 inches apart in rows or sections. Plant at the depth recommended on the seed packet. Some seeds need to be on or near the surface, while others sprout better in the dark beneath a soil layer. After seeding, pat down the soil where each cluster was planted.

3. When seedlings sprout and grow their first true leaves, thin each cluster, leaving only the strongest plant. As plants grow and begin to crowd each other out, remove every other plant so that the remaining ones have plenty of space, light, and air circulation.

4. Mulching plants when they're 1½ to 2 inches high will help maintain an even soil temperature and moisture level as well as discourage weed growth. Mulch may not be the best answer if you have a slug, snail, or earwig problem. They are attracted to mulch and baby plants.

Some gardeners, especially those in areas with long, cold winters, like to get a head start on spring by starting these species indoors in late winter, then transplanting them into the garden as young plants. And if seed is the only way to obtain them, you'll definitely want to start

STARTING SEEDS AHEAD INDOORS

1. Start seeds 6 to 12 weeks before the outdoor growing season begins. Use a sterile starting mix to avoid loss from "damping off."* Fill a shallow container that has holes in the bottom with the mix and smooth gently. Sprinkle the seeds, either in rows or by broadcasting evenly over the surface of the mix about ¼-inch apart. If you are planting seeds in small individual pots, plant 2 to 3 seeds in each (keep only the strongest one once they sprout). Cover with more mix to the depth recommended on the seed packet.

2. Place the entire container in an inch or so of water. Be careful to keep the water level below the rim of the container. Leave it in the water for a half hour or so, allowing enough time for the water to seep up through to the surface of the starting mix. Remove the container from the water tray and allow the excess to drip out. Place the container where it will get at least 8 to 10 hours of light a day. You may have to supplement natural light with artificial light from grow lamps. Find a spot where the soil will be kept warm or use a heater cable, since soil warmth is important.

3. When the seedlings sprout, the first leaves to appear are known as the "seed leaves."

* *"Damping off" is a fungus infection that strikes very young seedlings, causing them to simply lie down and die. It is best avoided by making sure that both the soil and the containers in which seeds are planted are sterile.*

the slower-growing and more difficult to germinate herbs (marjoram, lavender, rosemary, rue, and wormwood) in advance of the summer growing season. Most annuals will be up in one to two weeks. Perennials take two weeks or longer.

No matter how you start seeds, be sure to label them so you know what has been planted where. Young seedlings can be difficult to identify correctly. It's easy to lose track of what you have.

4. Transplant the tiny plants into regular growing soil in individual small pots or space them a couple of inches apart in plant boxes. Lift the young plants from underneath with a table knife or a spoon. Holding the plants by their base, gently separate them. Place the roots into a hole you've made with your finger or the knife. Plant the young plants at the same depth they were in the starter mix. Grow them in these pots or plant boxes until you are ready to plant them in permanent locations.

HERBS PROPAGATED FROM SEED

Angelica	Hyssop
Anise	Lavender
Basil	Lavender-Cotton
Borage	Lemon Balm
Burnet	Lovage
Calendula	Marjoram
Caraway	Nasturtium
Catnip	Parsley
Chamomile	Rosemary
Chervil	Rue
Chives	Sage
Coriander	Savory, Summer
Dill	Sorrel, French
Fennel	Sweet Woodruff
Garlic Chives	Tansy
Horehound	Thyme
Horseradish	Wormwood

STARTING FROM CUTTINGS

Before taking cuttings, fill a container with a moist rooting medium—a mixture in which the cuttings will remain while they develop roots. Coarse sand used to be the standard rooting medium. Although it's still perfectly acceptable and widely used, there are now several other alternatives. A very good rooting medium is made by mixing perlite with an equal amount of either peat moss or vermiculite. Another alternative is made by combining one part polymer soil additive (that has already been expanded with water) with two parts peat moss.

STARTING FROM CUTTINGS

1. Mix the rooting medium thoroughly and moisten it. Fill the container to within ¼-inch of the rim with the mixture. It should be at least 3 inches deep. Some good rooting mixes are one part perlite to one part peat moss or vermiculite, one part polymer soil additive to two parts peat moss, or clean, coarse builder's sand.

2. Use a sharp knife to cut active growth tips from the parent plant. Cut just below the point where a leaf joins the main plant stem. The cut must be clean and smooth; if it isn't, try again below the next leaf up on the shoot. The finished cuttings should be 3 to 6 inches long. Dip the lower third of the stem into rooting powder.

3. With a knife or sharp fingernails, carefully remove all the leaves and leaf stems from the lower one-half to two-thirds of the cutting stem. Avoid leaving shreds or tears as these provide sites for rot, which will kill cuttings before they can root. If the remaining leaves are very large, trim off a few more lower ones to prevent excessive water loss through the leaves.

To take cuttings, use a sharp knife to cut 3- to 6-inch-long growth tips from the parent plant. Make a clean cut immediately below the point where a leaf attaches to the main stem. Avoid crushing the stem, which is essential for the cutting's survival while it has no roots. If you make a mistake, recut below another leaf higher up on the shoot. Carefully remove all leaves and leaf stems from the bottom one-half to two-thirds of the cutting.

Although the use of a rooting hormone powder is not absolutely necessary, it does improve the success rate, especially for those herbs (such as lavender and

4. Poke a hole in the moist rooting medium with a knife blade or pencil. Insert the lower two-thirds of the cutting stem into the hole, making sure there are no leaves below the surface. Pack rooting medium firmly around the cutting stem. When all the cuttings are inserted, water from above to further settle the medium. Allow excess water to run out through the bottom holes.

5. Check the rooting progress every seven to ten days by gently lifting a cutting. When roots are ¼-inch long, plant them into regular potting soil in a small pot. Firm the soil around the stem and water from above after planting. Grow the cuttings in pots for at least six to eight weeks before moving them to a final site in the garden or to a larger container.

6. If plants are in peat pots, dig a hole in the prepared garden bed and drop plant, pot and all, into the hole. If plants are in pots, be sure the plant soil is moist. Hold pots upside down with the plant stem between two fingers and knock the pot edge sharply against something solid. The soil ball will fall out into your hand. Plant at the same depth as in the pot. Firm the soil around the roots, form a soil dam in a circle around plant stem, and fill the dam with water or mild fertilizer solution.

rosemary) that are more diffi-cult to root. Dip the lower third of the cutting into the

Potted herbs (clockwise from right): sage, rosemary, oregano, mint, and chamomile.

powder, then gently tap the base of the cutting against the inside of the packet to shake off excess powder.

Ideally, no more than 15 to 20 minutes should elapse from the time that a cutting is re-moved from the parent plant to the time it's inserted into the rooting medium. If this is impossible, to keep the cut-tings healthy and receptive to rooting, place them in water during the interim and plant them as soon as possible.

With a knife blade or pen-cil, poke a hole in the moist rooting medi-um and insert the bottom two-thirds of the cutting into the hole. Use your fingers to firm the med-ium around the cutting stem. Insert addi-tional cuttings into the medi-um with enough space between each so that the leaves just touch. Over-crowding will inhibit air circulation, which in turn will encourage the growth of undesirable fungi.

When all of the cuttings have been inserted, water the surface of the medium from above to further firm it around the cutting stems. Avoid get-ting water on the cutting leaves. Be sure to keep the soil damp continuously while rooting the cuttings. Place the container where there is a generous amount of light, but no direct sun. Be sure to keep the rooting medium very moist. After a week to ten days, check to see if any roots have appeared. Insert a knife blade beneath one of the cuttings and gently lift it out of the medium. If there are no visible roots, carefully reinsert the cutting and firm the medium around it; check again in another seven to ten days. Some plants take six or more weeks to root. Once the roots are ¼-inch long, plant them into a small pot.

Cover any large holes in the bottom of the pot with a paper towel or small stones. Fill the pot with either a moist commercial potting mix or your own homemade mixture of moist soil. Check the encyclopedia section to see what kind of soil each herb prefers, then use the appropriate mix recipe found on page 16. Poke a hole in the center of the soil with your fingers. Carefully lift the rooted cutting from the rooting medium in order to retain as many fragile roots and as much of the adhering medium as possible. Insert the rooted cutting into the hole. Firm the soil and water the

INDOOR AIR CIRCULATION

Outdoors, plants are exposed to air currents of all sorts, and many seem to need a certain amount of air movement indoors, as well. Air circulation helps ventilate waste gases, remove excess heat, and prevent diseases that can develop in closed spaces. There is often adequate air circulation near large windows because of temperature differences between day and night, but elsewhere, especially under plant lights, it's wise to run a small fan to keep the air in constant movement. Don't direct the fan on the plants— just having it in the same room will provide the needed circulation.

soil surface gently from above. Since excess water will drip out of the hole in the bottom of the pot, provide a drip tray. Don't allow plants to stand in water for more than two hours.

For at least a week or two, keep the potted cutting out of direct sunlight to avoid wilting. Grow it as a potted plant for at least a couple of months before tapping it out of the pot and planting it into a garden bed or a larger container.

The best time to take cuttings is during the mid-growing season, usually late spring or early summer, before the herbs have flowered.

STARTING BY LAYERING

Another method of propagation is layering. This method is suitable for most perennials with strong stems. Herbs in the mint family are the easiest ones for the beginner to layer, although hyssop, oregano, rosemary, and lavender also work well.

Select an outer stem from the plant's base and gently push it down to the earth. Mound a pile of dirt on top of the stem, leaving at least five inches of the stem end uncovered. Pack the soil tightly and water the mound well. Continue keeping the soil well watered for several weeks.

Every few weeks, check for the appearance of roots.

STARTING BY LAYERING

1. Select an outer stem from the base of a plant that has strong, flexible stems. Gently push the stem down to the ground.

2. Mound a pile of garden soil on top of the stem, leaving at least five inches at the end of the stem uncovered. Pack the soil tightly and water well.

3. Place a small rock over the mound of soil to keep the stem from springing back to an upright position. Keep the soil well watered for the next several weeks.

When they appear, make a quick, clean cut through the stem using a shovel or trowel to separate the layered herb from the original plant. Repot the new plant, being careful not to disturb the roots. Keep the new potted herb in a bright area away from direct light. In a couple of months, new leaves will start developing. Once they are well established, transplant the plant into a larger pot or into the garden.

Keep in mind that the harder the stem, the better chance of propagation. If the stem is woody, carefully wound the part of the stem that will be embedded in the soil. Gently score it with a trowel or knife to strip the bark. This will bring the nutrients in the soil directly to the stem quickly and efficiently.

For older plants with rigid central shoots, try mounding dirt around the base of the plant until only younger shoots protrude. This method works best in the spring and should produce rooted shoots ready for replanting by late summer. Most varieties of mint, thyme, and hyssop are especially receptive to this propagation method.

4. When roots appear, take a sharp shovel or trowel and make a quick, clean cut through the stem to separate the layered herb from the "mother" plant.

5. Lift the new little plant out of the ground and repot it. Be careful to disturb the roots as little as possible. Place the potted herb in a protected area in semi-shade or filtered light until it develops a sturdy root system.

HERB CHART

NAME	PLANT	LANDSCAPE	LIGHT	SOIL	HEIGHT (INCHES)	SPREAD (INCHES)	CULTURE
ANGELICA	B	✓	○ ◑	A,M	60-72	36	⬤
ANISE	A		○	A,D	18-24	4-8	⬤
BASIL	A	✓	○	R,M	18	10	⬤
BORAGE	A,B	✓	○	P-A	24-30	18	⬤
BURNET	P		○	A	18	12	⬤
CALENDULA	A	✓	○	A	12-24	12	⬤
CARAWAY	B		○ ◑	A,D	24	8	⬤
CATNIP	P		○ ◑	A-S	18-24	15	⬤
CHAMOMILE	P		○	A-P,D	9-12	4-6	⬤
CHERVIL	A		◑	A,M	18	4-8	⬤ ⬤
CHIVES	P	✓	○ ◑	A-R,M	8-12	8	⬤
CORIANDER	A		○	R	24-36	6	⬤
COSTMARY	P		○ ◑	R	30-36	24	⬤
DILL	A		●	A-S,M	24-36	6	⬤
FENNEL	P		●	R	50-72	18-36	⬤
GARLIC CHIVES	P		●	A-P	18	8	⬤
GERANIUMS, SCENTED	P	✓	●	A-R	VARIES	VARIES	⬤
HOREHOUND	P	✓	●	A-P	30	12	⬤
HORSERADISH	P		●	A	36-60	18-24	⬤
HYSSOP	P	✓	○ ◑	A	18	12	⬤
LAVENDER	P	✓	●	S,P	36-48	18-30	⬤

■ **PLANT** A /ANNUAL B /BIENNIAL P /PERENNIAL
■ **LIGHT** ○ /FULL SUN ◑ /PARTIAL SUN ● /SHADE
■ **SOIL** P /POOR A /AVERAGE R /RICH S /SANDY M /MOIST D /DRY
■ **CULTURE** ⬤ /EASY TO GROW ⬤ /AVERAGE ⬤ /DIFFICULT ⬤ /RAMPANT GROWER: KEEP RESTRICTED

NAME	PLANT	LANDSCAPE	LIGHT	SOIL (INCHES)	HEIGHT (INCHES)	SPREAD	CULTURE
LAVENDER-COTTON	P	✓	●	S.P	12-18	18	●
LEMON BALM	P		●◐	A-S,M	48	18	● ●
LOVAGE	P	✓	●◐	R,M	60	30	●
MARJORAM	P,A		●	R	8-12	12-18	●
NASTURTIUM	P,A	✓	●◐	A-P,M	12-72	18	●
OREGANO	P		●	A-S	18	12	●
PARSLEY	B	✓	●◐	R,M	12	8	●
PEPPERMINT	P		●◐	R,M	24-30	12	● ●
ROSEMARY	P	✓	●	S	48-72	18-24	●
RUE	P	✓	●	P,S	24	18	●
SAGE	P	✓	●	S	20	24	●
SAVORY, SUMMER	A		●	R-A	18	8	●
SORREL, FRENCH	P		●◐	R,M	18	10	●
SOUTHERNWOOD	P	✓	●	ANY	30	24	●
SPEARMINT	P		●◐	R,M	20	12	● ●
SWEET WOODRUFF	P	✓	●	R,M	6-8	6-8	●
TANSY	P		●◐	A-P	40	12-18	● ●
TARRAGON	P	✓	●◐	S-R	24	24	●
THYME	P	✓	●◐	P-A	1-10	12-18	● ●
WORMWOOD	P	✓	●	ANY	30-48	15-20	●

■ PLANT   A/ANNUAL B/BIENNIAL P/PERENNIAL
■ LIGHT   ● FULL SUN ◐ /PARTIAL SUN ● /SHADE
■ SOIL   P/POOR A/AVERAGE R/RICH S/SANDY M/MOIST D/DRY
■ CULTURE   ● /EASY TO GROW ● /AVERAGE ● /DIFFICULT ● /RAMPANT GROWER: KEEP RESTRICTED

Herbs in Containers and in the Garden

Although herbs are often planted in a very formal layout separate from the rest of the garden, this is by no means a requirement for success in growing them. Herbs can be mixed into other plantings. The exception is those few herbs such as mint, which will aggressively take over if not curbed. These are best planted in containers or separate beds, where strict control of their spread can be maintained.

An informal herb garden, such as this one in Maine, engenders tranquility.

33

Herbs can be laid out in a very formal or an extremely informal design or anywhere in between. The choice is entirely up to your tastes.

When planning a garden that includes herbs, the same basic rules of good design apply as when designing any other garden. Tall plants may be located at the rear of side beds, plants of intermediate height in the middle of the bed, and low-growing plants at the front. This way they'll all be visible and will obtain a maximum share of the available light. In central beds that are viewed from all sides, the tallest plants may be located in the center of the bed, the shortest plants around the outer edge, and the intermediate heights between the two.

Formal herb gardens keep alive a tradition that traces the course of human history.

Because so many herbs have inconspicuous flowers, the beauty of their foliage and its color and texture become important design factors. Herbs with silver-gray, blue-gray, or purple foliage become dramatic accents among the greens. Those with fine, fernlike leaves add a soft, airy look.

Even though all of these traits should be taken into consideration in your garden design, don't feel intimidated or overwhelmed by these details. Go ahead and lay out a plan to the best of your ability; then implement the plan without worrying that it must be "perfect." After all, you can always make adjustments in the future. Changing the details of a garden after it has been created is a fairly simple matter. In many cases, you can lift plants and move them to a new location without harming them.

The best approach to laying out a garden is to start by making a list of your favorite plants that you'd like to grow. Then write down their soil, light, and water needs; their height and spread; and any special notes—such as foliage type or color, flower color, or

HERBS BEST SUITED FOR CONTAINER GROWTH

Basil
Calendula
Catnip
Chives
Geraniums, Scented
Lavender
Lavender-Cotton
Marjoram
Oregano
Parsley
Peppermint
Rosemary
Rue
Sage
Savory, Summer
Sorrel, French
Spearmint
Thyme
Wormwood

unusual growth habit (consult the herb encyclopedia section for this information). Make a secondary list of those plants that you might enjoy having if there's any room left.

This formal garden emulates traditional English herb gardens of the seventeenth century.

Sketch the garden area to scale (that is, 1 inch on the sketch equals 1 foot on the ground, or some other suitable proportion), decide on the size and shape of the planting beds, and determine the locations of the plants on your list. Once all of the varieties on your favorites' list have been used, fill in any empty spots with appropriate species from your secondary list.

Be sure to consider the natural features of your garden, including its topography and the presence of any trees or shrubs. These factors will influence the amounts of light and water available to your garden. For example, small hills and valleys can interfere with sunlight and water runoff. More delicate herbs should not be placed in such a valley because they will probably receive too much water, though other herbs, such as peppermint and spearmint, will thrive in moist, soggy soil. Consider also the placement of taller plants in relation to smaller ones when planting on a hill. If the afternoon sun is blocked from smaller plants on a downslope by larger uphill plants, those smaller plants will receive much less light, and their growth will be affected. Allowing for these variances may prevent a lackluster growing season.

Also worth consideration is whether any permanent structures, such as a bench, walkway, or arbor, will be added. If so, then you may need to allow corridors in your garden layout for convenient access to these fixtures. A brick-paved pathway leading to a wooden bench near a focal point will add an almost decadent character to your garden. These accents are great for highlighting specific aspects of a garden and can transform an ordinary back yard into a conservatory.

The merits of an informal herb garden include a casual grace and natural simplicity.

SOME CLASSIC FORMAL HERB GARDEN DESIGNS

Classic designs replicate the formal, balanced geometric layouts favored by wealthy Europeans of past centuries. They usually revolve around some sort of special garden feature, such as a fountain, sundial, garden seat, statue, an unusual feature plant, or birdbath. All paths and attention lead to this feature, whether it's in the center of the garden or along one edge.

MONUMENT **WALL/ FENCE** **LOW- GROWING** **MEDIUM- GROWING** **TALL- GROWING**

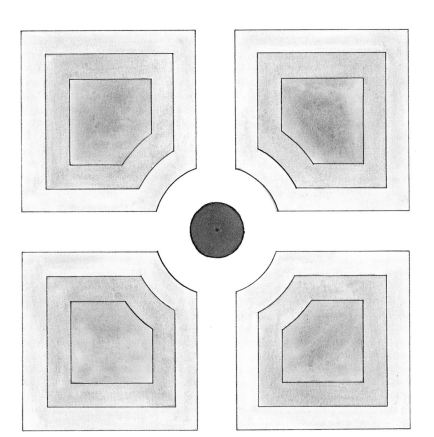

GROUP ONE—LOW

Dwarf Basil
Chamomile, Roman
Chives
Geraniums, Scented
Lavender, Munstead
(trimmed)
Lavender-Cotton
(trimmed)
Marjoram
Parsley
Rosemary, Creeping
(trimmed)
Sweet Woodruff
Thyme

GROUP TWO—MEDIUM

Anise
Basil
Burnet
Calendula
Caraway
Chervil
Coriander
Dill
Garlic Chives
Lavender-Cotton
Nasturtium
Rue
Sage
Savory, Summer
Tarragon

GROUP THREE—TALL

Angelica
Costmary
Fennel
Horseradish
Lavender
Lemon Balm
Lovage
Rosemary
Southernwood
Tansy
Wormwood

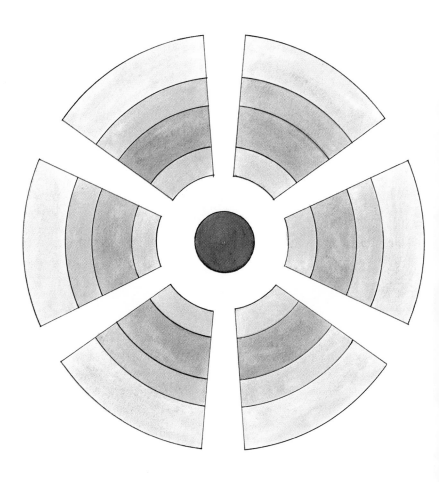

MONUMENT **WALL/ FENCE** **LOW- GROWING** **MEDIUM- GROWING** **TALL- GROWING**

INVASIVE PLANTS

Catnip
Chamomile
Chives
Costmary*
Garlic Chives
Horseradish*
Lemon Balm
Oregano
Peppermint*
Southernwod*
Spearmint*
Tansy*
Thyme

*Worst offenders that require containment; others can be more easily kept in bounds by frequent removal of excess growth.

Herbs are easily incorporated into a variety of landscape designs, and complement most statuary.

SOME INFORMAL HERB GARDEN LAYOUTS

Here are two informal layouts. One stands as an island in the middle of a lawn area, and the other backs a wall or fence.

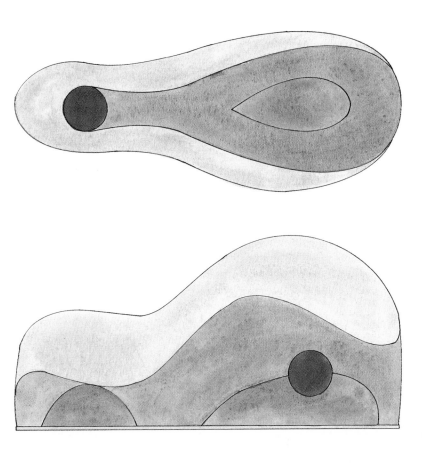

MONUMENT **WALL/ FENCE** **LOW- GROWING** **MEDIUM- GROWING** **TALL- GROWING**

HERBS TO CHOOSE FROM

These layouts are planned so you can follow them in a do-it-yourself manner. Simply mark those herbs you like best in each of the three lists on page 39, then plug them into the spaces in the designs that match their group number. For example, if your favorites in Group One are thyme and chives, plant them in each space that is marked "low-growing" on the plan you're following.

Combining herbs of various spreads and heights lends a robust look to an informal garden.

Arranging your garden like the one above yields a very full effect, with tall, medium, and short plants placed alongside one another.

This type of garden layout adds a more formal and structured air, with plants neatly arranged on the basis of their growth habits.

Harvesting, Preservation, and Storing

As a general rule of thumb, herbs have the highest level of flavor in their leaves just before they come into bloom. Therefore, harvests are best taken at this time. The various methods of preservation will influence the aromatic and textural characteristics of your harvest, so be sure to consider your purposes before preserving. In the herb encyclopedia section you'll find notes regarding the best time to harvest each herb listed as well as the best methods of preservation.

Preserving herbs from your garden allows for many decorative and culinary uses.

The most common method of herb preservation is by hang drying. Often, more fragile herbs such as calendula petals and chamomile blossoms are dried by spreading them in a thin layer on a piece of clean wire screening. Another good way to preserve many culinary herbs is by freezing them. It's very quick and easy, and the flavor is usually closer to fresh than dried. If you have the freezer space available, freezing is probably the most desirable choice for cooking herbs.

Once preserved, herbs are a wonderful way to make flavored oils and vinegars, which are decorative in themselves.

Some herbs lose flavor when exposed to air, but they will retain it if stored in oil or liquor. Another way to capture herbal flavors is by extracting the essential oils from the plant leaves and stems through distillation. This latter method is not easily done at home, but it's possible to purchase these essential oils from specialty suppliers and health food stores when you want them.

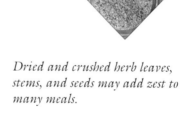

The steps to follow for drying, freezing, and storing herbs are provided in this chapter along with step-by-step illustrations. In every case, the most important point is to pick the herbs at their peak, process them, and properly store them as quickly as possible. Delays will inevitably result in loss of essential flavors and perfumes.

Dried and crushed herb leaves, stems, and seeds may add zest to many meals.

You'll note that some herbs don't retain as much flavor when preserved by any means—they can only be used fresh. You can, however, extend their season by growing them indoors as potted plants during the winter months. Not only will you have fresh herbs on hand for cooking or decorating, you will also have a fragrant reminder of what awaits at winter's conclusion.

HARVESTING

Harvesting of herbs for fresh use can be done throughout the growing season. When harvesting herbs to preserve for future use, wait until the plant is at its aromatic peak.

Harvest early in the morning when aromatics are at their highest level of the day. Though, be sure to wait until the plants have had at least an hour of sunlight to warm them and bring their aromatic oils out toward the leaves. Avoid any diseased or insect-infested portions.

If there is dust present, wash the plant thoroughly. If harvesting from the wild, be very certain that you've properly identified the plant to be picked. Many poisonous plants may grow alongside harmless herbs. Also make sure the area where you are harvesting is free from pesticides or other chemicals.

When harvesting roots, such as those of angelica, caraway, coriander, and horseradish, the best time to dig them up is in the fall.

Herbs are best harvested in the morning hours to ensure peak freshness.

Allow perennials at least two growing seasons before harvesting their roots to ensure adequate maturation. Be careful not to bruise the root—aromatic compounds are easily lost. Be careful when harvesting seeds. The timing must be precise to allow the seeds to ripen completely, but they must be caught before they disperse. One way to solve this problem is to keep watch on a daily basis and to pick as soon as the seeds begin to dry. Carefully snip off the heads over a large paper bag, allowing them to fall directly into it. Let them remain in the bag to dry. Be sure to harvest the seeds of annuals to ensure further propagation. Also remember to harvest those seeds with culinary uses such as caraway, coriander, dill, fennel, and lovage.

If you cannot keep such close track of the maturation process, another alternative is to enclose each seed head while still on the plant in a small paper bag once all flowering has ended and the green seeds become obvious. Then, when the heads dry, any seeds that fall out will be captured in the bag. Once the seeds are being released, snip off the heads, bag and all, and dry them indoors.

Once harvested, follow the step-by-step preservation instructions given on the following pages. But again, be sure you know how you'll use your herbs so you can follow the appropriate preservation method.

DRYING

To dry fresh herbs, as well as fresh flowers you might use in arrangements, first gather fresh branches of perennials or the entire annual plant in the early morning. Wash them thoroughly with plain water only if there is dust on them, since washing increases the loss of aromatics. Shake off as much water as possible; if the foliage is especially dense, pat it dry with towels.

The best location for drying herbs is in a dark place that is well ventilated, hot, and dry. An attic, barn, or shed loft; breezeway; or covered porch are good choices. Under these conditions, moisture will quickly evaporate from the plant materials while most of the important aromatic oils remain. Avoid drying herb leaves, stems, and flowers in a conventional oven: They will lose their aroma, taste, and delicacy.

DRYING HERBS

Method 1: Group herb and flower branches into small bunches for rapid drying with good air circulation to avoid the possibility of mold growth. The size of the bunch will depend on your local humidity (more sprigs per bunch in areas of low humidity and vice versa). Bind the stems together with an elastic band and hang them upside down in a hot, dry location with little or no light.

Method 2: Remove petals from flowers and leaves from stems, spreading them thinly on a tray made of clean screening. Leave space between the pieces for ventilation. Place the screen tray in a hot, dry location with little or no light and out of the wind, but where air can reach it from the bottom and top.

Method 3: Spread separate petals and leaves on a layer of paper towels. Place them in a microwave oven. Set on low for just one minute at a time; check often for degree of dryness. Remove them from the oven before they are fully dry and allow them to air-dry to avoid the possibility of overdrying.

Depending on the weather conditions, especially humidity, leaf and stem thickness, and other such variables, it will take anywhere from a day to a week to naturally air-dry various herbs. Check every day to see how the drying is progressing. There is a delicate balance between drying herbs too quickly and not quickly enough. If dried too rapidly, moisture and aromatic oils are drawn out of leaves or stems completely, leaving the herbs devoid of flavor. If dried too slowly, the risk is that the harvested herbs will decompose and lose essential oils through natural decay before the drying process locks them in.

As soon as the leaves are fully dry, but before they become brittle, strip them from the stems and store them in airtight containers to preserve as much flavor and aroma as possible. Label the containers to indicate their contents.

Method 4 (for seeds): Hang-dry bundles of plants as in Method 1, but place each bundle inside of a large brown paper bag that will catch the seeds. Alternatively, hang the bunches from poles laid across the open top of a large cardboard box that is lined with a sheet of paper.

Method 5 (for roots): Thoroughly scrub roots and split very thick ones lengthwise. Slice them into ¼-inch-thick pieces. Air-dry as in Method 2 or spread them on cookie sheets to dry in a regular oven at the lowest setting. Once the roots are brittle, place them in airtight containers for storage.

FREEZING AND OTHER METHODS OF PRESERVATION

The preliminary steps in preparing herbs for freezing are identical to those for drying. First gather fresh stalks and branches early in the morning when they have the highest concentration of aromatic oils. Wash them thoroughly in cool water to remove all dust, only if necessary. Remember that washing increases the loss of aromatics. Shake off as much water as possible; pat dry with towels.

For bouquet garni, break herbs into small sprigs; for addition to soups, stews, and other recipes, snip them into pieces with scissors or chop them with a knife or in a food processor. Mint or scented

PRESERVING HERBS

Freezing (Method 1): Separate herbs into small shoots or separate leaves; chop them as desired with a knife or scissors. Pack them in screw-top jars or sealable plastic bags with as little air as possible, and immediately put them in the freezer for storage.

Freezing (Method 2): Place the herb pieces in a blender or food processor with an equal amount of water. Chop them to desired size, pour them into ice cube trays, and freeze. You can also freeze whole leaves or flowers in ice cubes. When solid, transfer the cubes to storage containers and immediately return them to the freezer.

Candying: Pick and air-dry the stems, leaves, and flowers to be candied on paper towels. In a saucepan, add 1 cup sugar to ½ cup water. Cook on low heat, stirring, until clear. Partly cool and stir in 4 teaspoons of gum arabic. Chill. Dip each item into the chilled mix, using your finger to spread it over the entire surface. Place the pieces on a cake rack to dry, turning them once after 12 hours. When totally dry, store them in tightly covered containers.

geranium leaves can be frozen whole, then removed and floated unthawed in punches and other cold drinks. Use candied leaves and flowers for garnishes because most frozen leaves become limp as they defrost.

Specialty Notes:

Peel, then chop or grate horseradish root to a fine paste and loosely pack it in small jars; stir in a mix of 1 teaspoon salt dissolved in 1 cup of white vinegar. Be sure to stir out any air pockets. The herbs should be totally submerged. Prepare fresh ginger root the same way; combine and cover it with whiskey. Mix and cover peeled whole garlic cloves with vegetable oil.

Salting: In a stoneware crock, alternate a ½-inch layer of fresh, chopped herbs and a ½-inch layer of non-iodized salt. Pound the herbs with a wood mallet or jar to eliminate air spaces. Both the herbs and the salt can be used for seasoning any time after the first month. (Also see pages 62–63 for making herb vinegars and oils and pages 64–65 for pesto and bouquet garni recipes.)

HERBS TO FREEZE

Angelica	Nasturtium
Anise	Oregano
Basil	Parsley
Chervil	Peppermint
Chives	Rosemary
Coriander	Sage
Costmary	Savory,
Dill	Summer
Fennel	Sorrel,
Garlic	French
Chives	Spearmint
Lovage	Tarragon
Marjoram	Thyme

STORING HERBS

Careful storage of herbs is just as important as careful preparation and preservation. If any of these procedures is neglected, the end result will be loss of the essential oils—the source of an herb's flavor and perfume. Once the herbs are fully dry, there should be no delay in getting them stored in airtight containers with as little air space inside as possible. Also, ground or powdered herbs do not store as well as chopped herbs.

Containers suitable for storage of dried herbs include glass jars with tight-sealing lids or glass stoppers; tin canisters that can be tightly closed; plastic pill holders with tight covers; and sealable plastic bags, buckets, or barrels for large pieces. Frozen herbs should be stored in any tightly sealed plastic, glass, or metal container.

STORING HERBS

1. As soon as the herbs are dry but before they crumble when touched, remove the leaves, flowers, or seeds into a bowl. Leave them whole or crush them into a powder with a mortar and pestle.

2. Using a clean sheet of paper rolled into a funnel, pour the prepared herbs into containers.

3. Clean and dry the bowl, mortar, and pestle before processing the next variety. Label the container clearly with the name of the herb along with the year of harvest. Without labels it quickly becomes difficult to keep inventories straight.

Store them in a dark place in order to best preserve good color and flavor. If herbs must be stored in a lighted location, they should be kept in metal tins or dark-colored jars that will block out most or all of the light. Last but not least, clearly label each container with its contents and the date of harvest. Once frozen, it may become difficult to differentiate between one herb and another, and after several seasons of harvest, it's impossible to remember what year different herbs were preserved.

A good practice is to discard to the compost pile any remaining supply of an herb that has lost its zest. By promptly rotating out the surplus each season, you'll have full-strength herbs on hand at all times, as well as provide nutrient-rich waste for your compost pile.

4. Store herbs in a dark place to preserve colors and flavors. If no such space is available, store them in tins with tight covers or in sealable jars made from dark-colored glass. Rotate out any surplus left from the previous season as soon as the new supply is available.

5. To store large pieces of herbs suitable for use in herbal baths and herb wreaths, lay thoroughly dried branches in large plastic bags. Seal the open end tightly with an elastic band. Store in a dark place or inside a cardboard box. Large pieces can also be stored in large plastic buckets or fiberboard barrels with tight-fitting lids.

Cooking with Herbs

Nothing more effectively transforms bland menu staples into delicious culinary delights than the addition of your favorite herbs. Homemade soups, stews, vegetables, and bread come alive with flavor simply with the addition of herbs. Once you've had some success cooking with them, you'll become increasingly open to the idea of using herbs to vary your menu. With experience, you'll learn which herbs work with one another and just the right combinations to bring suprising zest to your meals.

Your herb garden will infuse your recipes with added flavor.

The ethnic favorites of many nationalities differ primarily in the combination and amounts of herbs and spices that are added, rather than in the varieties of meats as the kinds of olives, tomatoes, cooking oils, wines, cheeses, and hot and sweet peppers used. The flavors, nonetheless, are frequently very different. The Greeks add sage and licorice-flavored anise to their dishes, the Italians often use basil and oregano, the French prefer tarragon and rosemary, the Yugoslavs add paprika and poppy seeds, while the Spaniards favor bay leaves and saffron. The point is that seemingly small variations in the amounts and kinds of herbs and spices used will produce tremendous differences in the flavor of the finished product.

Subtle herb flavors define many regional variations in ethnic cooking.

and vegetables used. For example, Spain, France, Italy, Yugoslavia, and Greece have similar climates and foods available, and they cook these foods in similar ways. Obviously there is much overlap, and there are other important ingredient differences such

To taste the sparkle herbs add to your everyday favorites, simply mix a few chopped chives, dill, garlic chives, or caraway seeds into cream cheese or cottage cheese and use as a cracker spread. If you're still not convinced, sprinkle a dash of salt, oregano, and tarragon along with a splash of white vinegar over canned chickpeas; kidney, green, or wax beans; canned asparagus; or any steamed or boiled vegetable leftovers. Serve cold as a tasty side dish. Adjust the proportions to your own taste, and remember that a little goes a very long way when using these strong-flavored and aromatic ingredients. Substitute sage and marjoram for the oregano and tarragon and see how the flavor changes. Experiment with other combinations to discover which ones you and your family like best.

Several basic recipes are included here. We hope you'll use them as a foundation on which to build. We've also included a few more extravagant recipes to try once cooking with herbs becomes more familiar. There are no hard and fast rules of combination or proportion; the ones provided here are those that have been found to have a broad appeal.

Our chart on pages 84–85 lists those herbs most frequently recommended to complement a number of basic foodstuffs: different meats, vegetables, beverages, baked goods, and fruits. Each time you prepare one of these foods, add a different one of the herbs listed and see what you think of the result. Write down the amount and kind of herb you used, and whether or not you liked it. Over time, you'll learn which herbs you enjoy most and the proportions you prefer.

OILS AND VINEGARS

Best herbal oil choices:

Rosemary	Savory
Dill	Basil
Thyme	Coriander
Fennel	Marjoram
Tarragon	Mint
Garlic Chives	

Best herbal vinegar choices:

Basil	Chive Blossom
Dill	Garlic Chives
Tarragon	Savory
Thyme	Rosemary
Marjoram	

HERBAL OILS AND VINEGARS

Herb-flavored vinegars and oils are amazingly easy to make. Always start with a wine vinegar that has a pleasing flavor, since the original taste can only be altered, not improved, by the addition of herbs.

For an attractive appearance, select glass jars and bottles that have appealing colors and shapes. In addition to pleasing aesthetics, it's a great way to recycle glass bottles. Thoroughly clean and then sterilize recycled containers by steaming or boiling for 15 minutes. If food odors persist, discard the container.

Each herb flavor may be identified by inserting a fresh sprig into the bottle before filling it with herbal vinegar.

HERBAL OIL

1. Chop fresh, clean herbs and pack them loosely in a clean glass container, about one-third to one-half full. Fill the jar with room temperature oil. Cap the container and place it in a warm location. Stir or shake daily for three to five days.

2. Remove herbs by pouring them through a cheesecloth or a fine sieve. Test for flavor. Repeat the process with a new batch of fresh herbs if the flavor of the oil is too mild.

3. Pour the finished product into small bottles and jars with tight-sealing caps. Label and date.

You can also use written labels or tie a color-coded yarn around the bottle necks.

Since herbal oils have a higher concentration of flavor than vinegars, they're added to recipes in much smaller amounts. Therefore, for the best flavor, store herbal oils in small containers and keep them tightly sealed.

High quality olive oil is best, but any flavorless cooking or salad oil, such as safflower or sunflower oil, can be used. As with vinegars, a strong-flavored oil will overpower subtle herb flavors, so be careful in your selection.

For both oils and vinegars, if after standing for two weeks the flavor is not as strong as preferred, strain the existing mixture to remove herbs. Then add fresh herbs.

HERBAL VINEGAR

1. Pour vinegar over fresh, clean, chopped herbs loosely packed in a large glass container. Use all of one variety or mix herbs, whichever you prefer. Fill the jar about one-third to one-half full with herbs and add vinegar to the top. Cap the container securely with an acid-resistant lid. Keep it at room temperature. Stir or shake well once each day for two weeks.

2. Taste a sample for flavor. Pour the vinegar through cheesecloth to strain out the herbs. Add plain vinegar to dilute it if the taste is too strong.

3. For decoration and identification, you can insert a sprig of fresh herb into each sterilized storage bottle, but this is optional. Pour herbal vinegar into a bottle and cap tightly. Cork stoppers can be sealed by dipping the jar top into melted paraffin wax once the stopper is securely in place. Label and date the vinegar.

BOUQUET GARNI

For use in sauces or soup stocks, bouquet garni can be sprinkled directly into a pot or, for clear stock, enclosed in a clean cloth bag and removed from the liquid at the end of cooking time.

Recipe 1
Using Fresh or Frozen Ingredients

  1 ¼ CUPS FIRMLY PACKED
            LIGHT BROWN SUGAR
    3 SPRIGS PARSLEY OR
           CHERVIL OR BOTH
  ½ BAY LEAF
    2 SPRIGS THYME
    1 STALK CELERY

Recipe 2
Using Dried Ingredients

    1 TEASPOON DRIED PARSLEY
  ⅛ TEASPOON THYME
  ⅛ TEASPOON MARJORAM
  ¼ BAY LEAF
  ¼ TEASPOON CELERY SEED

Variation

For winter squash or sweet potatoes: Use equal parts angelica and bay leaves.

FINES HERBES

Fines herbes are used in egg and cheese dishes, soups, and sauces. Mince fresh or frozen herbs together; to retain full flavor, add them at the last minute before removing the dish from heat and serving.

    Basic Ingredients: equal parts of parsley, chervil, and chives

    Optional Additions: thyme, tarragon, savory, or basil

PESTO

Pesto may be added to soups and stews as is. It may also be blended with milk, cream, or wine to make a sauce for pasta, fish, chicken, or fresh vegetables.

Basic Recipe
1 ½ TO 2 CUPS FRESH OR
    FROZEN HERB LEAVES*
2 LARGE CLOVES GARLIC
½ CUP FRESHLY GRATED
    PARMESAN CHEESE
2 TEASPOONS FRESHLY
    GRATED ROMANO
    CHEESE
½ CUP OLIVE OIL
½ CUP PINE NUTS OR
    WALNUTS
    SALT AND PEPPER TO
    TASTE

    Combine herbs, garlic, and cheeses in food processor. Turn on the processor and slowly add oil and nuts. Blend until a paste is formed. Season to taste. Pour into a glass container with a ¼-inch skim of plain oil on top and cover tightly. Store in refrigerator.

Variation
You can leave out the cheeses and garlic and freeze the pesto in serving-size portions. To do so, spoon the pesto into ice cube trays, freeze, remove promptly, and permanently store in tightly sealed freezer containers. Add cheeses and garlic when thawed and ready to use.

* Use any one of the following quantities and combinations:

Option 1: 2 cups basil

Option 2: 1 cup basil and 1 cup watercress

Other options: ½ cup oregano, savory, sage, tarragon, or thyme and 1½ cups parsley

FRESH TOMATO PASTA ANDREW

2 main-dish or 4 appetizer servings

- 1 POUND FRESH TOMATOES, CUT INTO WEDGES
- 1 CUP PACKED FRESH BASIL LEAVES
- 1 TABLESPOON EACH FRESH OREGANO AND PARSLEY LEAVES
- 2 CLOVES GARLIC
- 2 TABLESPOONS OLIVE OIL
- 8 OUNCES CAMENZOLA CHEESE OR 6 OUNCES RIPE BRIE PLUS 2 OUNCES STILTON CHEESE, EACH CUT INTO SMALL PIECES
- SALT AND WHITE PEPPER TO TASTE
- 4 OUNCES UNCOOKED ANGEL HAIR PASTA, VERMICELLI OR OTHER THIN PASTA, HOT COOKED AND DRAINED
- GRATED PARMESAN CHEESE

Place tomatoes, basil, oregano, parsley, garlic, and oil in covered food processor or blender; pulse on and off until ingredients are coarsely chopped, but not pureed. Combine tomato mixture and Camenzola cheese in large bowl. Season to taste with salt and white pepper. Add pasta; toss gently until cheese melts. Serve with Parmesan cheese. Garnish as desired.

Favorite recipe from California Fresh Market Tomato Advisory Board

BEEF FAJITAS

4 to 6 servings

- ¼ CUP LIME JUICE
- ¼ CUP TEQUILA
- 2 TABLESPOONS VEGETABLE OIL
- 2 CLOVES GARLIC, MINCED
- 1 FRESH OR CANNED JALAPEÑO PEPPER, STEMMED, SEEDED, AND MINCED
- 1 TEASPOON EACH CHOPPED FRESH PARSLEY, CILANTRO, AND CHIVES
- ¼ TEASPOON SALT
- ¼ TEASPOON GROUND BLACK PEPPER
- 1½ POUNDS BEEF FLANK STEAK
- 2 CANS (ABOUT 16 OUNCES EACH) REFRIED BEANS
- 8 TO 12 FLOUR TORTILLAS, 8-INCH DIAMETER

CONDIMENTS
- 2 AVOCADOS
- LIME JUICE
- SALSA
- SOUR CREAM

To prepare marinade, combine lime juice, tequila, oil, garlic, jalapeño pepper, parsley, cilantro, chives, salt, and black pepper in small bowl. Trim any visible fat from meat; place in heavy, self-sealing plastic bag. Pour marinade over meat; seal bag. Refrigerate 8 hours or up to 2 days, turning bag occasionally to distribute marinade.

Preheat charcoal grill and grease grill rack. Place refried beans in large skillet and heat through; keep warm. Stack and wrap tortillas in foil; place tortillas on side of grill to heat. Remove meat from marinade; reserve marinade. Place meat on grill 4 to 6 inches above solid bed of coals (coals should be medium-glowing). Cook, basting frequently with reserved marinade, 4 minutes on each side for rare or until meat is brown on the outside but still pink when slashed in thickest part. To serve, cut meat across the grain into thin slices; place on warm platter. Peel, pit, and chop avocados; sprinkle with lime juice. Place tortillas, refried beans, avocados, salsa, and sour cream in separate serving dishes. Wrap the meat and condiments in tortilla and eat out of hand.

FORTY-CLOVE CHICKEN FILICE

1 (3-POUND) FRYING
    CHICKEN, CUT INTO
    SERVING PIECES
40 CLOVES GARLIC (ABOUT
    2 HEADS*)
1 LEMON
1 ½ CUPS DRY WHITE WINE
¼ CUP DRY VERMOUTH
¼ CUP OLIVE OIL
4 RIBS CELERY, THICKLY
    SLICED
2 TABLESPOONS FINELY
    CHOPPED PARSLEY
2 TEASPOONS DRIED BASIL
    LEAVES, CRUSHED
1 TEASPOON DRIED
    OREGANO LEAVES,
    CRUSHED
  PINCH OF CRUSHED RED
    PEPPER FLAKES
  SALT AND BLACK PEPPER
    TO TASTE

The whole garlic bulb is called a head.

1. Preheat oven to 375°F. Place chicken, skin side up, in single layer in shallow baking pan; set aside.

2. Peel whole heads of garlic; set aside.

3. To prepare lemon, hold lemon in one hand. With other hand, remove colored portion of peel with vegetable peeler or zester into small bowl. To juice lemon, cut lemon in half on cutting board; with tip of knife, remove visible seeds. Using citrus reamer or squeezing tightly with hand, squeeze juice from lemon into small glass or dish; remove any remaining seeds from juice.

4. Combine garlic, wine, vermouth, oil, celery, parsley, basil, oregano, and red pepper flakes in medium bowl; mix thoroughly. Sprinkle garlic mixture over chicken. Place zest over and around chicken in pan; pour lemon juice over top of chicken. Season with salt and black pepper.

5. Cover pan with foil. Bake 40 minutes.

6. Remove foil; bake 15 minutes or until chicken is tender and juices run clear. Garnish as desired.

Makes 4 to 6 servings

CHICKEN WITH LIME BUTTER

3 WHOLE CHICKEN BREASTS, SPLIT, SKINNED, AND BONED
$\frac{1}{2}$ TEASPOON SALT
$\frac{1}{2}$ TEASPOON PEPPER
$\frac{1}{3}$ CUP VEGETABLE OIL
1 LIME
$1\frac{1}{2}$ CUPS BUTTER, SOFTENED
1 TEASPOON MINCED FRESH CHIVES
$\frac{1}{2}$ TEASPOON DRIED DILL WEED, CRUSHED
LIME SLICES, QUARTERED CHERRY TOMATOES, AND DILL SPRIGS FOR GARNISH

1. Sprinkle chicken with salt and pepper.

2. Heat oil in large skillet over medium heat. Add chicken to skillet in single layer. Cook 6 minutes or until chicken is light brown, turning once. Cover; reduce heat to low. Cook 10 minutes or until chicken is tender and no longer pink in center. Remove chicken to serving platter; keep warm.

3. Drain oil from skillet.

4. To juice lime, cut lime in half on cutting board; with tip of knife, remove any visible seeds. Using citrus reamer or squeezing tightly with hand, squeeze juice from lime into skillet; remove any remaining seeds from skillet.

5. Simmer lime juice over low heat 1 minute or until juice begins to bubble.

6. Stir in butter, 1 tablespoon at a time, until sauce thickens.

7. Remove sauce from heat; stir in chives and dill weed.

8. Spoon sauce over chicken. Garnish, if desired.
Makes 6 servings

RACK OF LAMB WITH DIJON–MUSTARD SAUCE

1 RACK OF LAMB
   (3 POUNDS), ALL
   VISIBLE FAT REMOVED
1 CUP FINELY CHOPPED
   FRESH PARSLEY
½ CUP DIJON-STYLE
   MUSTARD
½ CUP SOFT WHOLE WHEAT
   BREAD CRUMBS
1 TABLESPOON CHOPPED
   FRESH ROSEMARY OR
   2 TEASPOONS DRIED
   ROSEMARY
1 TEASPOON MINCED GARLIC

1. Preheat oven to 500°F. Place lamb in large baking pan.

2. Combine parsley, mustard, bread crumbs, rosemary, and garlic in small bowl. Spread evenly over top of lamb. Place in center of oven; cook 7 minutes for medium-rare. Turn off oven but do not open door for at least 30 minutes.

3. Serve 2 to 3 chops on each plate, depending on size and total number of chops. Serve with Rosemary Bread Sticks (recipe on page 77). Garnish with additional fresh rosemary, lemon slices, and lemon peel strips, if desired. *Makes 6 servings*

LEMON TOSSED LINGUINE

- **8** OUNCES UNCOOKED LINGUINE NOODLES
- **3** TABLESPOONS FRESH LEMON JUICE
- **2** TEASPOONS REDUCED CALORIE MARGARINE
- **2** TABLESPOONS MINCED CHIVES
- **1/3** CUP SKIM MILK
- **1** TEASPOON CORNSTARCH
- **1** TABLESPOON MINCED FRESH DILL OR **1** TEASPOON DRIED DILL WEED
- **1** TABLESPOON MINCED FRESH PARSLEY OR **1** TEASPOON DRIED PARSLEY
- **2** TEASPOONS GRATED LEMON PEEL
- **1/4** TEASPOON GROUND WHITE PEPPER
- **3** TABLESPOONS GRATED ROMANO OR PARMESAN CHEESE

1. Cook noodles according to package directions, omitting salt; drain well. Place in medium bowl; pour lemon juice over noodles.

2. Meanwhile, melt margarine in small saucepan over medium heat. Add chives and cook until chives are soft. Combine milk and cornstarch and stir into saucepan. Cook and stir until thickened. Stir in dill, parsley, lemon peel, and white pepper.

3. Pour milk mixture over noodles. Sprinkle with cheese; toss to coat evenly. Serve immediately.

Makes 6 (1/2-cup) servings

CROSTINI

¼ LOAF WHOLE WHEAT
  BAGUETTE (4 OUNCES)
4 PLUM TOMATOES
1 CUP (4 OUNCES) SHREDDED
  PART-SKIM MOZZARELLA
  CHEESE
3 TABLESPOONS PREPARED
  PESTO SAUCE

1. Preheat oven to 400°F. Slice baguette into 16 very thin, diagonal slices. Slice each tomato vertically into four ¼-inch slices.

2. Place baguette slices on nonstick baking sheet. Top each with 1 tablespoon cheese, then 1 slice tomato. Bake about 8 minutes or until bread is lightly toasted and cheese is melted. Remove from oven; top each crostini with about ½ teaspoon pesto sauce. Garnish with fresh basil, if desired. Serve warm.

Makes 8 appetizer servings

HERBED GREEN BEANS

1 POUND FRESH GREEN
  BEANS, STEM ENDS
  REMOVED
1 TEASPOON EXTRA VIRGIN
  OLIVE OIL
2 TABLESPOONS CHOPPED
  FRESH BASIL *OR*
  2 TEASPOONS DRIED
  BASIL LEAVES

1. Steam green beans 5 minutes or until crisp-tender. Rinse under cold running water; drain and set aside.

2. Just before serving, heat oil over medium-low heat in large nonstick skillet. Add basil; cook and stir 1 minute, then add green beans. Cook until heated through. Garnish with additional fresh basil, if desired. Serve immediately.

Makes 6 servings

MARINATED ARTICHOKES & SHRIMP IN CITRUS VINAIGRETTE

VINAIGRETTE

- 1 LARGE SEEDLESS ORANGE, PEELED AND SECTIONED
- 3 TABLESPOONS RED WINE VINEGAR
- 3 TABLESPOONS FAT FREE MAYONNAISE
- 1 TEASPOON FRESH THYME OR 1/4 TEASPOON DRIED THYME LEAVES
- 2 TEASPOONS EXTRA VIRGIN OLIVE OIL

SALAD

- 1 PACKAGE (9 OUNCES) FROZEN ARTICHOKE HEARTS, THAWED
- 12 RAW SHRIMP (12 OUNCES)
- 1 CUP ORANGE JUICE

1. To prepare vinaigrette, place all vinaigrette ingredients except oil in blender or food processor; process until smooth. Pour mixture into medium nonmetal bowl and whisk in oil until well blended. Fold artichoke hearts into vinaigrette. Cover and refrigerate several hours or overnight.

2. Peel shrimp, leaving tails attached. Devein and butterfly shrimp. Bring orange juice to a boil in medium saucepan. Add shrimp and cook about 2 minutes or just until they turn pink and opaque.

3. To serve, place about 3 artichoke hearts on each of 6 plates. Top each serving with 2 shrimp. Drizzle vinaigrette over tops. Garnish with fresh Italian parsley, if desired.
Makes 6 appetizer servings

WHOLE WHEAT HERB BREAD

⅔ CUP WATER
⅔ CUP SKIM MILK
2 TEASPOONS SUGAR
2 ENVELOPES ACTIVE DRY YEAST
3 EGG WHITES, LIGHTLY BEATEN
3 TABLESPOONS OLIVE OIL
1 TEASPOON SALT
½ TEASPOON EACH DRIED BASIL LEAVES AND DRIED OREGANO LEAVES
4 TO 4½ CUPS WHOLE WHEAT FLOUR

1. Bring water to a boil in small saucepan. Remove from heat; stir in milk and sugar. When mixture is warm (110° to 115°F), add yeast. (Water at higher temperatures will kill the yeast.) Mix well; let stand 10 minutes or until bubbly.

2. Combine egg whites, oil, salt, basil, and oregano in large bowl until well blended. Add yeast mixture; mix well. Add 4 cups flour, ½ cup at a time, mixing well after each addition, until dough is no longer sticky. Knead about 5 minutes or until smooth and elastic, adding more flour if dough is sticky. Form into a ball. Cover and let rise in warm place about 1 hour or until doubled in bulk.

3. Preheat oven to 350°F. Punch dough down and place on lightly floured surface. Divide into 4 pieces and roll each piece into a ball. Lightly spray baking sheet with nonstick cooking spray. Place dough balls on prepared baking sheet. Bake 30 to 35 minutes until golden brown and loaves sound hollow when tapped with finger.
Makes 24 slices

CORN AND TOMATO CHOWDER

1 ½ CUPS PEELED AND DICED PLUM TOMATOES
¾ TEASPOON SALT, DIVIDED
2 EARS CORN, HUSKS REMOVED
1 TABLESPOON MARGARINE
½ CUP FINELY CHOPPED SHALLOTS
1 CLOVE GARLIC, MINCED
1 CUP CHICKEN BROTH
1 CAN (12 OUNCES) EVAPORATED SKIM MILK
¼ TEASPOON BLACK PEPPER
1 TABLESPOON FINELY CHOPPED FRESH SAGE OR 1 TEASPOON RUBBED SAGE
1 TABLESPOON CORNSTARCH
2 TABLESPOONS COLD WATER

1. Place tomatoes in nonmetal colander over bowl. Sprinkle ½ teaspoon salt on top; toss to mix well. Allow tomatoes to drain at least 1 hour.

2. Meanwhile, cut corn kernels off the cobs into small bowl. Scrape cobs, with dull side of knife, to "milk" liquid from cobs into same bowl; set aside. Discard 1 cob; break remaining cob in half.

3. Heat margarine in heavy medium saucepan over medium-high heat until melted and bubbly. Add shallots and garlic; reduce heat to low. Cover and cook about 5 minutes or until shallots are soft and translucent. Add broth, milk, black pepper, sage, and reserved corn cob halves. Bring to a boil over high heat. Reduce heat to low; simmer, uncovered, 10 minutes. Remove and discard cob halves. Add corn; return to a boil over medium-high heat. Reduce heat to low; simmer, uncovered, 15 minutes more.

4. Dissolve cornstarch in water; add to chowder, mixing well. Stir until thickened. Remove from heat; stir in drained tomatoes and remaining ¼ teaspoon salt. To serve, spoon into bowls. Garnish with additional fresh sage, if desired.

Makes 6 appetizer servings

PORK LOIN ROASTED IN CHILI-SPICE SAUCE

1 CUP CHOPPED ONION
1/4 CUP ORANGE JUICE
2 CLOVES GARLIC
1 TABLESPOON CIDER VINEGAR
1 1/2 TEASPOONS CHILI POWDER
1/4 TEASPOON DRIED THYME LEAVES
1/4 TEASPOON GROUND CUMIN
1/4 TEASPOON GROUND CINNAMON
1/8 TEASPOON GROUND ALLSPICE
1/8 TEASPOON GROUND CLOVES
1 1/2 POUND PORK LOIN, FAT TRIMMED
3 FIRM LARGE BANANAS
2 LIMES
1 RIPE LARGE PAPAYA, PEELED, SEEDED, CUBED
1 GREEN ONION, MINCED

1. Preheat oven to 350°F. Combine onion, orange juice, and garlic in food processor; process until finely chopped. Pour into medium saucepan; stir in vinegar, chili powder, thyme, cumin, cinnamon, allspice, and cloves. Simmer over medium-high heat about 5 minutes or until thickened.

2. Cut 1/4-inch-deep lengthwise slits down top and bottom of roast at 1 1/2 inch intervals. Spread about 1 tablespoon spice paste over bottom; place roast in baking pan. Spread remaining 2 tablespoons spice mixture over sides and top, working mixture into slits. Cover. Bake 45 minutes or until meat thermometer registers 140°F.

3. Remove roast from oven; increase oven temperature to 450°F. Pour off liquid; discard. Return roast to oven and bake, uncovered, 15 minutes or until spice mixture browns lightly and meat thermometer registers 150°F in center of roast. Remove from oven; tent with foil and let stand 5 minutes before slicing.

4. Meanwhile, spray 9-inch pie plate or cake pan with nonstick cooking spray. Peel bananas and slice diagonally into 1/2-inch-thick pieces. Place in pan. Squeeze juice from 1 lime over bananas; toss to coat evenly. Cover; bake in oven while roast stands or until hot. Stir in papaya, juice of remaining lime, and green onion.

Makes 6 servings

ROSEMARY BREAD STICKS

⅔ CUP **2%** LOW FAT MILK
¼ CUP FINELY CHOPPED
    FRESH CHIVES
2 TEASPOONS BAKING
    POWDER
1 TEASPOON FINELY
    CHOPPED FRESH
    ROSEMARY OR DRIED
    ROSEMARY
¾ TEASPOON SALT
½ TEASPOON BLACK PEPPER
¾ CUP WHOLE WHEAT FLOUR
¾ CUP ALL-PURPOSE FLOUR
    NONSTICK COOKING SPRAY

1. Combine milk, chives, baking powder, rosemary, salt, and black pepper in large bowl; mix well. Stir in flours, ½ cup at a time, until blended. Turn onto floured surface and knead dough about 5 minutes or until smooth and elastic, adding a little more flour if dough is sticky. Let stand 30 minutes at room temperature.

2. Preheat oven to 375°F. Spray baking sheet with cooking spray.

3. Divide dough into a 12 equal balls, about 1¼ ounces each. Roll each ball into a long thin rope and place on prepared baking sheet. Lightly spray bread sticks with cooking spray.

4. Bake about 12 minutes or until bottoms are golden brown. Turn bread sticks over and bake about 10 minutes more or until other side is browned.

Makes 12 bread sticks

GRILLED VEGETABLES

1/4 CUP MINCED FRESH HERBS,
   SUCH AS PARSLEY,
   THYME, ROSEMARY,
   OREGANO, OR BASIL
1 SMALL EGGPLANT (ABOUT
   3/4 POUND), CUT INTO
   1/4-INCH-THICK SLICES
1/2 TEASPOON SALT
   NONSTICK COOKING SPRAY
1 EACH RED, GREEN, AND
   YELLOW BELL PEPPER,
   QUARTERED AND
   SEEDED
2 ZUCCHINI, CUT
   LENGTHWISE INTO
   1/4-INCH-THICK SLICES
1 FENNEL BULB, CUT
   LENGTHWISE INTO
   1/4-INCH-THICK SLICES

1. Combine herbs of your choice in small bowl; let stand 3 hours or overnight.

2. Place eggplant in large colander over bowl; sprinkle with salt. Drain 1 hour.

3. Heat grill until coals are glowing red, but not flaming. Spray vegetables with cooking spray and sprinkle with herb mixture. Grill 10 to 15 minutes or until fork-tender and lightly browned on both sides. (Cooking times vary depending on vegetable; remove vegetables as they are done to avoid overcooking.)

Makes 6 servings

Variation:

Cut vegetables into 1-inch cubes and thread onto skewers. Spray with cooking spray and sprinkle with herb mixture. Grill as directed above.

GRILLED SCALLOP CEVICHE

6 TO 7 OUNCES SEA SCALLOPS, 1 TO 2 INCHES IN DIAMETER

¼ CUP LIME JUICE, DIVIDED

¼ TEASPOON CHILI POWDER OR PAPRIKA

½ LARGE HONEYDEW MELON

1 RIPE MEDIUM PAPAYA OR MANGO, OR ½ LARGE CANTALOUPE

¼ CUP MINCED ONION

1 TO 2 FRESH JALAPEÑO OR SERRANO PEPPERS, SEEDED, MINCED

3 TABLESPOONS MINCED FRESH MINT OR FRESH BASIL

1 TEASPOON HONEY (OPTIONAL)

1. Rinse scallops and pat dry. Place scallops, 2 tablespoons lime juice, and chili powder in large resealable food storage bag. Marinate scallops in refrigerator 1 hour.

2. Scoop seeds from melon. Remove fruit with melon baller or cut melon into ¾-inch wedges; remove rind and cut fruit into cubes. Halve papaya, scoop out seeds, remove peel with knife; cut fruit into cubes. Place fruit into nonmetallic bowl. Stir in remaining 2 tablespoons lime juice, onion, and jalapeño. Cover and refrigerate.

3. Spray cold grid with non-stick cooking spray. Adjust grid 4 to 6 inches above heat. Preheat grill to medium-high.

4. Drain scallops; discard marinade. Thread scallops onto 10- to 12-inch metal skewers. Grill skewers 3 minutes or until marks are established. Turn skewers over; grill until scallops are opaque.

5. Remove scallops from skewers; cut into quarters. Stir into fruit mixture. Refrigerate until thoroughly chilled, about 30 minutes or up to 24 hours. Stir in mint and honey.
Makes 6 servings

MEDITERRANEAN FISH SOUP

4 OUNCES UNCOOKED PASTINA OR OTHER SMALL PASTA
NONSTICK COOKING SPRAY
¾ CUP CHOPPED ONION
2 CLOVES GARLIC, MINCED
1 TEASPOON FENNEL SEEDS
1 CAN (14½ OUNCES) NO-SALT-ADDED STEWED TOMATOES
1 CAN (14½ OUNCES) ⅓-LESS-SALT CHICKEN BROTH
1 TABLESPOON MINCED FRESH PARSLEY
½ TEASPOON GROUND BLACK PEPPER
¼ TEASPOON GROUND TURMERIC
8 OUNCES FIRM, WHITE-FLESHED FISH, CUT INTO 1-INCH PIECES
3 OUNCES RAW SMALL SHRIMP, PEELED AND DEVEINED

1. Cook pastina according to package directions, omitting salt. Drain and set aside.

2. Spray large nonstick saucepan with nonstick cooking spray. Add onion, garlic, and fennel seeds; cook over medium heat 3 minutes or until onion is soft.

3. Stir in tomatoes, chicken broth, parsley, black pepper, and turmeric. Bring to a boil, reduce heat and simmer 10 minutes. Add fish and cook 1 minute. Add shrimp and cook until shrimp just begins to turn opaque.

4. To serve, divide pastina among bowls; ladle soup over pastina.

Makes 4 (1½-cup) servings

PASTA SALAD

4 CUPS BROCCOLI
    FLOWERETS
2 CUPS CARROT SLICES
1 ½ CUPS CHOPPED TOMATOES
½ CUP CHOPPED GREEN
    ONIONS WITH TOPS
½ POUND SPIRAL PASTA,
    COOKED AND WELL
    DRAINED
1 CUP FAT FREE
    MAYONNAISE
2 TABLESPOONS WHITE WINE
    VINEGAR
1 TABLESPOON EXTRA VIRGIN
    OLIVE OIL
1 TABLESPOON MINCED
    FRESH BASIL OR
     1 TEASPOON DRIED
    BASIL LEAVES
2 TEASPOONS MINCED FRESH
    OREGANO OR
    ½ TEASPOON DRIED
    OREGANO LEAVES
1 CLOVE GARLIC, MINCED
1 TEASPOON SUGAR
1 TEASPOON DRY MUSTARD
¼ TEASPOON EACH SALT AND
    BLACK PEPPER
½ CUP (2 OUNCES) FRESHLY
    GRATED ROMANO
    CHEESE

1. Steam broccoli 3 minutes or until crisp-tender; immediately drain and run under cold water. Steam carrots 4 minutes or until crisp-tender; immediately drain and run under cold water. Combine broccoli, carrots, tomatoes, green onions, and pasta in large bowl.

2. Combine all remaining ingredients except cheese in small bowl; blend well. Stir into pasta mixture. Add cheese; toss well. Refrigerate 3 hours or overnight to allow flavors to blend.

Makes 8 servings

SALMON EN PAPILLOTE

³⁄₄ CUP WATER

1 TEASPOON EXTRA VIRGIN OLIVE OIL

¹⁄₄ TEASPOON SALT

¹⁄₈ TEASPOON BLACK PEPPER

¹⁄₂ CUP COUSCOUS
    PARCHMENT PAPER

1 SMALL YELLOW SQUASH, CUT INTO JULIENNED STRIPS (1 CUP)

¹⁄₂ POUND FRESH SALMON FILLET, BONES REMOVED AND CUT INTO 2 PIECES

¹⁄₂ CUP PEELED AND DICED PLUM TOMATOES

2 TEASPOONS EACH CHOPPED FRESH DILL AND CHOPPED FRESH TARRAGON OR ¹⁄₄ TEASPOON EACH DRIED DILL WEED AND DRIED TARRAGON LEAVES

2 TEASPOONS EACH CHOPPED FRESH CHIVES AND CHOPPED FRESH PARSLEY

1 EGG, BEATEN

DILLED WINE SAUCE

1 ¹⁄₂ CUPS FINELY CHOPPED ONIONS

1 TABLESPOON DRIED DILL WEED OR ¹⁄₂ CUP CHOPPED FRESH DILL

1 ¹⁄₄ TEASPOONS DRIED TARRAGON LEAVES OR ¹⁄₄ CUP CHOPPED FRESH TARRAGON

1 CLOVE GARLIC, PEELED AND QUARTERED

¹⁄₂ CUP DRY WHITE WINE

2 TEASPOONS EXTRA VIRGIN OLIVE OIL

1. Preheat oven to 350°F. To prepare couscous, combine water, oil, salt, and black pepper in small saucepan with tight-fitting lid. Bring to a boil. Add couscous and mix well. Cover and remove from heat. Let stand 5 minutes or until all liquid is absorbed.

2. Make 2 large hearts with 2 sheets parchment paper by folding each piece in half and cutting into half-heart shape. Unfold hearts and spoon ½ cup couscous on one side of each heart. Top each with ½ cup squash, 1 piece salmon, ¼ cup tomato, and 1 teaspoon each dill, tarragon, chives, and parsley. To seal packages, brush outer edges of hearts with beaten egg. Fold over again making half-heart shapes; press edges together, crimping tightly with fingers. Place packages on ungreased baking sheet; bake 14 minutes.

3. To prepare Dilled Wine Sauce, combine all ingredients except oil in blender or food processor; process until smooth.

4. Pour dill mixture into small saucepan and bring to a boil over medium heat. Reduce heat to low; simmer until reduced by half. Strain sauce into small bowl, pressing all liquid through strainer with back of spoon. Slowly whisk in oil until smooth and well blended

5. To serve, place each package on large plate and cut an "X" in top. Fold corners back and drizzle sauce over each serving. Garnish with edible flowers, such as pansies, violets, or nasturtiums, if desired.

Makes 2 servings

CULINARY HERB CHART

MEATS

BEEF
ANGELICA
CARAWAY SEEDS
CHIVES
CORIANDER SEEDS
HORSERADISH ROOT
MARJORAM
OREGANO
SAGE
SAVORY, SUMMER
SORREL, FRENCH

VEAL
BASIL
CHERVIL
CHIVES

LAMB
BASIL
DILL
HYSSOP
PEPPERMINT
ROSEMARY
SAGE
SORREL, FRENCH
SPEARMINT

PORK
ANGELICA STEMS
CARAWAY SEEDS
DILL
MARJORAM
OREGANO
ROSEMARY
SAGE

POULTRY
BASIL
BORAGE FLOWERS
CALENDULA PETALS
CHIVES
CORIANDER SEEDS
DILL
HYSSOP

LOVAGE SEEDS
MARJORAM
OREGANO
PARSLEY
ROSEMARY
SAGE
TANSY
TARRAGON
THYME

SEAFOOD

SHELLFISH
BASIL
CHIVES
CORIANDER
COSTMARY
DILL
OREGANO
THYME

FISH
ANISE SEEDS
BASIL
BORAGE FLOWERS
CARAWAY SEEDS
CHERVIL
CHIVES
COSTMARY
DILL
FENNEL
HORSERADISH ROOT
MARJORAM
PARSLEY
ROSEMARY
SAGE
SAVORY, SUMMER
TANSY
TARRAGON
THYME

VEGETABLES

TOMATOES
BASIL
DILL
LOVAGE SEEDS

OREGANO
ROSEMARY
SAGE
SAVORY, SUMMER
TARRAGON

POTATOES
BASIL
CARAWAY SEEDS
CHIVES
CORIANDER
DILL
FENNEL SEEDS
HORSERADISH ROOT
LOVAGE SEEDS
MARJORAM
OREGANO
PARSLEY

SALADS
ANISE
BASIL
BORAGE FLOWERS
BURNET
CALENDULA PETALS
CARAWAY
CHERVIL
CHIVES, LEAVES,
    FLOWERS
CORIANDER ROOT
FENNEL
GARLIC CHIVES
GERANIUMS, SCENTED,
    FLOWERS
HORSERADISH ROOT
HYSSOP*
LEMON BALM
LOVAGE LEAVES,
    STEMS, SEEDS
NASTURTIUM LEAVES,
    FLOWERS
PARSLEY
ROSEMARY*
SAGE*

* SALAD SEASONING ONLY

SAVORY, SUMMER*
SORREL, FRENCH
TARRAGON*

PICKLES

BORAGE FLOWERS
CORIANDER SEEDS
DILL LEAVES, SEEDS
LOVAGE SEEDS
NASTURTIUM BUDS,
  FLOWERS, FLOWER
  BUDS, LEAVES
TARRAGON

CHEESE DISHES

COTTAGE CHEESE

ANISE
CARAWAY SEEDS
CHIVES
DILL
MARJORAM
OREGANO
PARSLEY
SAVORY, SUMMER
THYME

CHEESE SPREAD

BORAGE FLOWERS
BURNET
CALENDULA PETALS
CARAWAY SEEDS
CHIVES
CORIANDER SEEDS
DILL LEAVES, SEEDS
FENNEL SEEDS
GARLIC CHIVES
GERANIUMS, SCENTED,
  FLOWERS
LOVAGE SEEDS
MARJORAM
OREGANO
ROSEMARY
SAGE

EGG DISHES

CHERVIL
CHIVES
COSTMARY
FENNEL
MARJORAM
OREGANO
PARSLEY
ROSEMARY
TANSY
TARRAGON

SOUPS

ANGELICA
ANISE SEEDS
CALENDULA PETALS
CARAWAY LEAVES,
  ROOTS
CHERVIL
CHIVES
GARLIC CHIVES
HYSSOP
LOVAGE STEMS, LEAVES
MARJORAM
PARSLEY
ROSEMARY
SAGE
SAVORY, SUMMER
SORREL, FRENCH
THYME

STEWS

ANGELICA
ANISE SEEDS
BASIL
CARAWAY LEAVES,
  ROOTS
CHERVIL
CORIANDER SEEDS
DILL
LOVAGE
MARJORAM
SAGE
SAVORY, SUMMER

STUFFING

MARJORAM
SAGE
THYME

BAKED GOODS AND BREADS

ANGELICA ROOT,
  SEEDS, AND CANDIED
  STEMS
ANISE SEEDS
CARAWAY SEEDS
CORIANDER SEEDS
FENNEL SEEDS
GERANIUMS, SCENTED
ROSEMARY
SAGE
TANSY

BEVERAGES

WINE PUNCH

BURNET
CALENDULA PETALS
SWEET WOODRUFF

FRUIT DRINKS

BORAGE
COSTMARY
LEMON BALM
PEPPERMINT
SPEARMINT

TEA

ANGELICA ROOTS,
  SEEDS
ANISE SEEDS, LEAVES
CATNIP
CHAMOMILE FLOWERS
GERANIUMS, SCENTED
HOREHOUND
HYSSOP
PEPPERMINT
SAGE
SPEARMINT

* SALAD SEASONING ONLY

Decorating
with Herbs

Sprigs of herbs, whether fresh or dried, make aromatic and attractive additions to any home decor. The simplest way to enjoy them indoors is to cut stems of one or more varieties, arrange them in a vase, pitcher, or bean pot filled with water, and place them wherever a live accent is desirable. Another easy way to use fresh herbs is as a filler in fresh floral bouquets. Mint, curly parsley, basil, rosemary, sage, and southernwood are all good choices.

Dried herb decorations can add a simple charm no matter what their use.

Many herbs have decorative flowers. Calendulas have large daisylike blooms throughout the summer ranging from lemon-yellow to intense orange in color; borage produces brilliant blue, star-shaped blossoms; tansy blooms are a strong-scented mass of small, bright-yellow buttons; and lavender provides abundant blue spikes early each summer. Nasturtiums give the most outstanding display of all. They bloom abundantly right up until the first fall frost in a tremendous range of brilliant colors.

While stunning in the garden, this bold foliage is also great for inside the house. Dried herbs can be used in a number of different decorative ways. The easiest is to tie several fresh branches tightly together with ribbon or cloth complementary in color and texture and hang them upside down as sprays. They'll look great hanging individually or in groups in the kitchen, dining room, or pantry.

A more formal look, appealing to use in any room in the house, can be achieved by making an herb wreath, heart, or crescent. Wood, wire, or plastic foam base forms for these pieces can be found at most craft stores and florist shops, or you can make your own. Simply attach the herbs by firmly wrapping them onto the form with florist wire or

Herbs in any modest display can soften even the most urban landscape.

twine (those with stiff stems can simply be poked in if a plastic foam base is used).

Additional herbs, clusters of dried flowers, groups of whole spices such as nutmeg and cinnamon sticks, or decorative bows can be used to fill in any bare spots and to provide accents to the wreath once the foliage base is completed.

Mix foliages or make an entire wreath from a single variety. The fullness and impact of the wreaths will vary depending on the density and texture of the materials used. Wreaths made from bay leaves will look deep green, formal, sleek, and sculptured. Thyme produces a narrow, delicate, airy outline. Southernwood gives a heavy, dense, silvery result. Experiment with different varieties to suit your tastes.

HERBS FOR DRIED ARRANGEMENTS

Foliage	Seed Heads
Chervil	Dill
Chives	Rue
Lavender	
Lavender-Cotton	Flowers
Rosemary	Chives
Sage	Garlic Chives
Southernwood	Lavender
Thyme	Lavender-Cotton
Wormwood	Marjoram
	Oregano
	Tansy

Indoors, you may enjoy herbal aromatics through potpourris and sachets. Potpourri can be used to lightly scent the air anywhere in the house. Sachets delicately perfume closed spaces such as linen and clothes closets, bureau drawers, and hope chests. For the simplest aromatic of all, toss a few fresh or dried sprigs into the fireplace or float them in a shallow pan of water heating on a wood stove or cooktop. The pleasing aroma will instantly release to the entire house.

DECORATING WITH WREATHS AND BASKETS

Wreaths. Wreath backgrounds are favorites for creating dried floral designs. A huge variety is available in the marketplace with new choices being released yearly. When choosing a wreath base, consider the mood and feeling you wish your wreath to convey; then consider the types of dried flowers you will be working with. Size is important as well. Larger dried flowers should be placed on a larger wreath form. Small, delicate materials find a better home on a smaller, more delicate wreath base.

Baskets. A basket is a good choice as the container for a dried flower arrangement. Baskets are reasonably priced and there is no end to the shapes, sizes, textures, and fiber combinations available.

In some cases, baskets may present a problem. A tall

Wreath backgrounds are available in any number of colors, textures, and shapes.

basket, for example, will need some sort of weight in the base to keep it from toppling over. Simply place a large, flat stone, brick, bag of pebbles, or sand into the bottom of the basket before putting the foam inside. Other baskets may be slightly off balance due to packaging and shipping. Always check how the basket sits on a flat surface before purchasing it. Often, it can simply be pushed back into shape. However, if it does not stay, be careful. It may be difficult to work with and probably will be impossible to design correctly.

Baskets of both wicker and rattan make decorative containers for dried herbal arrangements.

Check the basket for uneven wicker ends that may snag or detract from the finished design. Be sure the handle is securely attached and will not loosen in time. If you purchase a basket that is off balance, hold it over a pot of steaming water for a minimum of five minutes or until you feel the fibers softening.

Place it on a flat surface to reshape. Hold it in place with a heavy weight until the fibers dry and become firm again. If they do not respond, repeat the entire process, steaming for a longer period of time until the basket stays as you want it.

For an immediate decorative and aromatic effect, simply bring freshly harvested herbs in from the garden and loosely arrange them in a basket. Place them near a window so their scents will permeate adjoining rooms. When the aroma begins to wane, just harvest more herbs.

MAKING AN HERB WREATH

Sooner or later, most herb gardeners find themselves with an excess supply of herbs. Rather than discarding the surplus of your harvest, try making an herb wreath. They are very easy to make and last for many years if kept away from direct sun and moisture.

If possible, it's best to use partially dried herbs. They're still pliable enough to handle without crumbling and yet stiff enough not to wilt after the wreath is completed. If fresh greens are used, mildew can result if they're too solidly packed together; if too loosely arranged, the wreath may look bare.

Different wreath bases can be used, depending on the look you desire. A ring of stiff, rippled wire produces a

MAKING AN HERB WREATH

1. Use hand pruners to cut partially dried herb branches into 5-inch pieces.

2. Use a spool of florist wire or twine to attach the plant materials to the wire base. Lay a bundle of two or three pieces of herb on top of the wire base, then wrap the twine firmly for three or four turns around both the base and the herb stems starting halfway down the stems and spiralling down toward the cut ends. Lay another bundle on top of the first one's stems, allowing the attractive section to show, and continue spiral wrapping until the form is filled.

3. Gently lift the first bundle of the circle in order to squeeze the last one or two bundles in. Flatten the lifted bundle back over the final ones by gently massaging it in place with your hand. Hang the wreath and adjust where needed: Add pieces to thin or narrow spots and thin or trim with pruning shears where the greenery is too dense or straggling.

narrow, flat wreath. A flat plastic foam circle will produce a fuller wreath of medium width. For a very full, rounded wreath use a base of plastic foam molded over a wire ring.

Shapes and sizes other than those available from a florist or craft shop can be made at home from plywood or a wire coat hanger. Grape vines, rope, woven rattan, and straw rings can all be used to create unique designs.

Stiff-stemmed herbs can be wrapped with florist wire or, in the case of plastic foam, pushed into the base. Those with weak or small stems should be gathered into small bundles and wired to a wooden stem or florist's pick (available at floral supply and many craft stores). They can then be handled the same as those with stiff stems.

Completed herbal wreaths are as varied as the greens that are used to make them. Use a single species or a mixture of herbs. Different combinations will look delicate and airy, dense and handsome, or just plain homey. They combine nicely with other dried materials such as baby's breath and statice, too. Be creative.

4. Leave the wreath lying flat until the herbs are completely dried out before hanging it up. This will avoid the possibility of the wreath becoming misshapen due to further drying. If desired, decorate the wreath further. Wreaths are also attractive when laid flat on a table. For example, you may use a wreath to surround a punch bowl or a candlestick base.

POTPOURRIS AND SACHETS

Potpourris are a mixture of sweet-scented petals, leaves, and spices that slowly release their perfume as an air freshener. They can be stored in a decorative airtight container and opened for brief periods as needed. When left open continuously, the aromatic properties are quickly lost, but do perfume the room.

Sachets are small packets of concentrated scent that can be slipped into bureau drawers or clothes and linen closets where they add a subtle fragrance to stored belongings.

Potpourris are quickly made, since the herbs, petals, and spices are simply stirred together and stored. A potpourri that is losing strength can often be revitalized by simply dropping two or three drops of essential oil into the container and covering it tightly for a few days. Sachets take a bit more work, as the ingredients are ground, then usually sewn or wrapped in fabric.

Sachet bags may be made from netting, silks, satins, and laces to add a feeling of opulent luxury. They can also be made from plain cottons or ginghams to echo a simple country theme. Fill them with basic blends of fragrant herbs, or use the potpourri mix described in this chapter.

The materials necessary to make a potpourri include lemon or orange peels, cinnamon, cloves, or allspice, and orris root. Orris root helps blend the aromas and enhance their intensity.

POTPOURRI AND SACHET MAKING

Angelica	Hyssop
Basil	Lavender
Chervil	Lavender-Cotton
Chives	Marjoram
Coriander	Rosemary
Costmary	Sweet Woodruff
Geraniums, Scented	Thyme
	Wormwood

POTPOURRI AND SACHET MAKING

1. Assemble dried herbs, citrus peels, spices, orris root powder, and essential oils. Combine the scents you find pleasing, using larger amounts of those with more delicate scents and smaller quantities of those that are strong scented. Add essential oils one drop at a time. Mix gently and thoroughly. Be very cautious as these oils can easily overpower any other ingredients.

2. When the blend suits you, mix in 1 tablespoon chopped orris root to each cup of mixture. This fixes the scent to make it last longer. Store for 6 to 8 weeks in an airtight container in a dark, dry place to allow the fragrances to blend.

3. Spoon the mixture loosely into a nice-looking container with a tight-fitting top. Set it in a convenient location where it can be opened to release its perfume whenever you like.

To make a sachet, just use a mortar and pestle to pound potpourri into a medium to fine powder. Spoon it into a bag made of tightly woven fabric and sew the bag securely shut.

HERBS FOR FRESH ARRANGEMENTS

Foliage
Angelica
Basil
Garlic Chives
Horehound
Lavender
Lavender-Cotton
Rue
Southernwood
Wormwood

Seed Heads
Caraway
Dill
Rue

Flowers
Borage
Calendula
Chives
Garlic Chives
Lavender
Lavender-Cotton
Nasturtium
Oregano
Tansy

HERBAL ARRANGEMENTS

Herbs make especially attractive additions to fresh or dried floral arrangements. Many have foliage of unusual texture, color, or both, adding visual interest and variety to any arrangement. Good examples are lush angelica, gray-green needled lavender, silvery knobbed lavender-cotton, purple basil, and densely ruffled parsley. They are also fragrant, giving an arrangement an added bonus. Since herbs are usually very long-lasting, they'll look great in a fresh flower arrangement for as long or longer than the flowers.

Most herbs are not well known for their flowers, but a few do have nice blooms for fresh use. These include nasturtium, borage, calendula, chamomile, oregano, tansy, lavender, and chives. The latter four also dry well for use in winter bouquets.

Also appealing are the flat umbel flowers of dill, caraway, and coriander. These make airy, starlike additions to arrangements while in bloom as well as later in the growing season when their green seedpods develop.

EUROPEAN HERB BASKET

1. In a large plastic-lined basket, place pots of assorted herbs. Experiment with the herbs you have available to find complementary colors and textures.

2. Add a container filled with floral foam in the basket so that cut flowers can be added. Add the cut flowers to the floral foam.

3. Cover the floral foam and pots with moss.

To speed herbal preservation in glycerine, slice the ends of the stems at an angle to increase the rate of absorption.

PRESERVING WITH GLYCERINE

Since herbs used in arrangements will not be eaten, an alternative way to preserve them is with glycerine. Mix together 1 part glycerine (available at most drugstores) and 2 parts hot water in a jar and stir well. Cut the fresh herb stems at an angle with a sharp knife or scissors and arrange them in the jar in 3 or more inches of liquid. Leave them in this solution, refilling the jar as the mixture is absorbed by the herbs.

You'll notice a color change as the glycerine slowly rises up into the leaves. After two weeks to a month when fully changed in color, remove the herbs from the solution.

Materials preserved this way stay pliable and remain useful for several years. Store them in a dry place so that the glycerine will not attract water.

Be sure to pick branches to be treated late in the season when they have full-sized leaves and mature, woody stems.

DESICCANTS

Desiccants are moisture-absorbing substances and include sand, borax, and silica gel. Sand has been used for centuries and the finest grade, available from many craft stores, is an excellent non-toxic desiccant and may find other purposes in your garden. (If you opt for silica or borax, be sure to keep it out of reach of children and pets.)

For drying flowers with a desiccant, choose a container made of glass or plastic, since wood or cardboard may retain water. Fill the container with about 1 inch of desiccant and add flowers. Lightly cover flowers and leaves; use a spoon for intricately textured petals. After 5-10 days, your flowers and leaves should be dried.

TUSSY MUSSIES

1. Tussy mussies are a lovely old-fashioned way to display and give away fresh herbs. Using an oasis holder (which can be purchased at craft stores), place a flower—a rosebud or a tansy cluster—in the center by inserting the stem into the oasis. Add additional small pieces of each kind of herb desired around the center, rotating as you work, until the arrangement is 2 to 4 inches across.

2. If you do not want to use an oasis holder, you may use a flower for the center and then add herbs around it. Wrap the stems together in floral tape, then place the bouquet inside a decorative paper doily, a ring of wilt-resistant leaves such as ivy, or a lace circle. Add a small ribbon bow, if you want more color.

Cosmetic Uses

For centuries, people have made cosmetic use of various aromatic and healthful essences derived from herbs. With the current enthusiasm for natural products instead of artificial, there has been a renewal of interest in herb-based perfumes, baths, soaps, powders, and astringents. Numerous specialty shops now offer a broad variety of herbal cosmetic products as well as ingredients for making your own.

Herbs can make aesthetic contributions of a more personal nature when used in cosmetics.

Unless you have a very large garden to provide a generous supply of the necessary herbs, as well as the equipment for distilling herbal oils, the most sensible approach may be to buy the ingredients you'll need to make your own products. Your local health supply store

One trip to a health supply store and a bountiful harvest in the garden can yield many natural cosmetics.

will probably stock most of what you need: scented waters, essential oils, dried herbs and flowers, powdered orris, and other herbal powders. Isopropyl rubbing alcohol, unscented talc, and a few herbal oils are available in many drugstores.

BATHS

The simplest method for preparing an herbal bath is to gather together several sprigs of one or more fresh or dried herb favorites and hold them under the tap while very hot water flows over them to fill the tub. To avoid having bits of leaves and flowers in the water, place the sprigs inside a fine-meshed drawstring bag and hang it under the tap or let it float in the water while the tub is filling. Squeeze the bag in the bathwater, setting it aside once the tub is filled. Discard the herbs and let the bag dry completely before using it again.

Another approach is to add just one or two drops of essential oil to the tap water as the tub is filling. Remember, these oils are highly concentrated so a little will go a long way.

Finally, herbs can be added to the tub in the form of bath salts. Mix together 2 parts regular baking soda, 1 part powdered orris root, and 2 to 3 drops of an herbal oil such as lavender or rosemary for every 3 ounces of soda/orris mixture. Mix well and store in an airtight container. Use one handful per bath.

DUSTING POWDERS

Body powders are easily made by adding very finely powdered herbs that have been sifted or a few drops of essential oils to a scentless talcum powder. A homemade powder made from 5 ounces powdered orris, 9 ounces cornstarch, and 2 ounces rice flour may be substituted for talcum powder. The powder can be made without orris root for those who may be allergic to it. When using essential oils, add 8 drops of oil, one drop at a time, to each pound of powder. Mix very thoroughly with a mortar and pestle to distribute

the oil evenly throughout the powder base.

THOSE HERBS MOST POPULAR FOR USE IN BATHS ARE:

Lavender

Rosemary

Marjoram

Parsley

Calendula Petals

Lovage

Mint

Basil

Hyssop

Chamomile

Scented Geraniums

Southernwood

Sage

Thyme

CLEANSING FACIAL STEAM

To create a pore-cleansing facial steam, simply add about 1 tablespoon of fresh or 1½ tablespoons of dry herbs to a quart of boiling water in a prewarmed bowl. Keeping your eyes closed, hang your face over the bowl and cover both your head and the bowl with a bath towel tent. Allow the vapor to rise around your face for about 5 to 10 minutes; if it becomes too uncomfortable, take a break by removing the tent for a minute, then continue the treatment. At the end of treatment, splash your face with lukewarm water, then with cold water. You may also use cotton balls to apply an astringent lotion if your skin is especially oily. These final steps are necessary to close the pores the steam opened.

POWDERS

Lavender and anise are favorite herbs to mix into powders. Other common spices popularly used include cloves, coriander, sandalwood, and mace.

ASTRINGENT FACIAL SCRUB

For those with oily skin, a cleansing facial scrub can be made by mixing dry oatmeal or cornstarch (as a thickener) to lemon juice or cider vinegar, mixed with dried sage, yarrow, or chamomile.

RINSES

To give a nice shine to your hair after washing it, you need to plan ahead. Prepare the rinse in advance, using a tablespoon of dried herbs to a quart of boiling water. Allow the mixture to steep for half an hour, then strain out the herbs and allow the rinse to cool. Pour this infusion over your hair as a final rinse after shampooing.

More specifically, to brighten light-colored hair, try this natural herbal rinse. Steep 2 tablespoons of dried chamomile and 2 tablespoons of dried marigold in 1 quart of boiled water for half an hour. Make certain the water is a comfortable temperature, then pour slowly through wet hair.

To burnish darker-colored hair, substitute sage and rosemary for the chamomile

---

RINSES

Herbs best suited for rinses are:
Calendula Petals
Chamomile
Rosemary
Parsley

and marigold called for above. For extra luster, add 1 tablespoon of cider vinegar; for more depth, add 1 tablespoon of strong dark tea.

PERFUMED TOILET WATERS

With patience and experimentation, it's possible to successfully produce a pleasant perfumed toilet water at home. Simply add a few drops of essential oil—lavender, rose, orange, and lemon are used frequently, but not exclusively—to a quart of isopropyl alcohol and shake together well every day for one week. Then pour into small, tightly closed bottles to retain the delicate fragrance. For a more astringent mixture, mix oils in witch hazel instead of alcohol. Try using various combinations of oils to create the fragrance that best suits your tastes and personality.

FACIALS

The best herbs for facials are:

Hyssop

Chamomile

Lavender

Scented Geraniums

Peppermint

Rosemary

Sage

Antique glass bottles are the perfect containers for your homemade perfumes.

Herb
Encyclopedia

In the following pages, 41 of the most common and popular herbs are described. Each profile includes a photograph and a written description of the plant's habit of growth; details of site preferences; propagation; the best harvest time; and methods of preservation and storage. There are also notes on the following uses for each species: culinary, decorative, and cosmetic. Since most herbs aren't noted for their blooms and many have inconspicuous or unimportant flowers, floral color is only noted for those few that have decorative blossoms.

Despite the numerous varieties of herbs cultivated, most are easily grown.

Angelica

BIENNIAL

BOTANICAL NAME: *Angelica archangelica*

HEIGHT: 60 to 72 inches

SPREAD: 36 inches

DESCRIPTION: This large, boldly attractive biennial has very lush growth. The flowers are white umbels followed by decorative yellow-green seedpods. Its flavor is licoricelike.

EASE OF CARE: Easy

HOW TO GROW: Angelica likes a cool, moist location and average to well-drained soil. It will grow in sun or partial shade. Sow seeds in place or transplant them when still very small as they don't like to be moved.

PROPAGATION: By seed. Seeds must be no more than a few weeks old to be viable. Sow in late fall or early spring while the ground is still cool. Leave seeds uncovered.

USES: *Fresh leaves*—soups, stews

Dried leaves—salads, soups, stews, potpourris

Fresh foliage—floral arrangements

Seeds—teas, baked goods

Stems—candy, pork, baked goods

Dried roots—teas, breads

Root oil—baths, lotions

PRESERVATION: Harvest stems during second spring, leaves throughout summer season, roots in fall, and seeds when ripe. Stems can be candied or frozen.

Anise

ANNUAL

BOTANICAL NAME: *Pimpinella anisum*

HEIGHT: 18 to 24 inches

SPREAD: 4 to 8 inches

DESCRIPTION: Feathery leaves and a lacy flower umbel are held on a tall and not very strong stem. These annuals look similar to dill and, like that plant, do best when grown closely together either in rows or clumps so that the multiple stems provide support for one another.

EASE OF CARE: Easy, but it will take at least 4 frost-free months to grow seeds to maturity. Therefore, in northern areas only the leaves can be obtained from home-grown plants.

HOW TO GROW: Plant in full sun and average to light, dry soil. Either seed in place where they'll grow or transplant them when small.

PROPAGATION: By seed in early spring.

USES: *Fresh or frozen leaves*—salads, cottage cheese, teas, jellies

Seeds—perfumes, soaps, breads, cookies, fish stocks, teas, soups, stews

PRESERVATION: Harvest leaves during late summer for freezing. Harvest seeds when fully ripe, watching carefully to cut plants at ground level when first seeds ripen. Hang-dry the seed heads inside paper bags in a warm, dry place.

Basil

ANNUAL

BOTANICAL NAME: *Ocimum basilicum*

HEIGHT: 18 inches

SPREAD: 10 inches

DESCRIPTION: Basil has a very neat, dense growing habit with attractive, glossy, bright-green, triangular leaves. All varieties of this good-looking annual make effective additions to any garden.

EASE OF CARE: Easy

HOW TO GROW: Full sun and rich, moist soil are preferred. Sow seeds when soil is warm, or get a head start by starting them indoors and transplanting after frost.

PROPAGATION: By seed outdoors in late spring or indoors 8 weeks before the last frost.

USES: *Fresh, dried, and frozen leaves*—vinegars, sauces, stews, salads, fish, shellfish, chicken, veal, lamb, tomatoes, potatoes

Dried leaves—potpourris and sachets

Fresh branches—floral arrangements

Cosmetic uses—hair rinses, toilet waters, soaps

PRESERVATION: The ideal harvest time is when flower buds are about to blossom. Prunings can be used whenever they are taken. Hang-dry and store in airtight containers; better flavor is retained if frozen or stored in oil or vinegar.

Borage

ANNUAL TO BIENNIAL

BOTANICAL NAME: *Borago officinalis*

HEIGHT: 24 to 30 inches

SPREAD: 18 inches

DESCRIPTION: A basal rosette of long, spear-shaped leaves produces tall stems covered with attractive, bright-blue, star-shaped flowers that hang downward. Borage is a nice addition to any flower garden. All parts of the plant are densely covered with hairs. The flavor is similar to cucumber. Although usually grown as an annual, this plant will often overwinter in mild climates for a second growing season.

EASE OF CARE: Easy

HOW TO GROW: Borage prefers a dry, sunny location in poor to ordinary, well-drained soil. It is difficult to transplant; move when very young if it must be moved at all.

PROPAGATION: By seed in early spring or late fall.

USES: *Fresh leaves*—fruit drinks

Flowers—salads, pickles, candy, cheeses, fish, poultry, vegetables, floral arrangements

PRESERVATION: Pick blossoms as they open and use them fresh or candy them. Leaves are good for fresh use at any time. Since much of the flavor is lost during drying, preserve as a flavored vinegar.

Burnet

PERENNIAL

BOTANICAL NAME: *Poterium sanguisorba*

HEIGHT: 18 inches

SPREAD: 12 inches

DESCRIPTION: A low, ground-hugging rosette of dark green leaves forms the basic plant from which 12- to 18-inch thin flower stems arise. This perennial is frequently grown as an annual in order to obtain the best flavor and most tender leaves. The flavor is that of cucumber.

EASE OF CARE: Easy

HOW TO GROW: Grow in full sun in average soil, although rich soil improves its flavor. Burnet prefers an alkaline soil; where soil is very acid, lime should be added. Young seedlings can be moved.

PROPAGATION: By seed; burnet will self-sow easily after the first planting.

USES: *Fresh leaves*—salads, wine punches, cheese spreads

PRESERVATION: Harvest leaves in early autumn and store them as flavored vinegar.

Calendula, Pot Marigold

ANNUAL

BOTANICAL NAME: *Calendula officinalis*

HEIGHT: 12 to 24 inches

SPREAD: 12 inches

DESCRIPTION: Very coarse, bright-green, strap-shaped leaves are held rather stiffly on the stems. Growth is brittle and snaps off fairly easily. This annual grows rapidly and blooms abundantly all summer until after the first frost. Flower colors range from bright yellow to vivid orange.

EASE OF CARE: Easy

HOW TO GROW: Calendulas enjoy full sun and average, well-drained soil. Sow them directly in the garden or start them early indoors for transplanting to the garden after the last frost. Insects like calendulas, so be careful.

PROPAGATION: By seed outdoors in the early spring or indoors 6 to 7 weeks before the last frost.

USES: *Fresh petals*—salads, soups, wine punches, cheeses, poultry

Dried petals—hair rinses, baths

Fresh flowers (complete)—floral arrangements

PRESERVATION: Remove petals from blossoms and spread them thinly on screening to dry. Grind them to a powder and store in an air-tight container.

Caraway

BIENNIAL

BOTANICAL NAME: *Carum carvi*

HEIGHT: 24 inches

SPREAD: 8 inches

DESCRIPTION: These biennials have finely cut leaves that strongly resemble carrot foliage. The white umbel flowers develop in the second year to produce flavored seeds.

EASE OF CARE: Average

HOW TO GROW: Caraway grows best in light, dry, well-drained soil in full sun, although it will tolerate partial shade. Mulching will provide the moist growing conditions caraway prefers. Plant in place as caraway does not transplant easily.

PROPAGATION: By seed outdoors in early spring or late summer.

USES: *Fresh leaves*—salads, soups, stews

Seeds—breads, sauerkraut, beef, pork, cheeses, potatoes, fish

Fresh root—use as a winter vegetable like parsnip in soups and stews

PRESERVATION: Harvest seeds when fully ripe, watching carefully to cut plants at ground level when first seeds ripen. Hang-dry the seed heads inside paper bags in a cool, dry place. Store in tightly sealed containers. In its first fall or spring, dig up roots, clean them, and store them in a root cellar or a similar root crop storage area.

Catnip, Catmint

PERENNIAL

BOTANICAL NAME: *Nepeta cataria*

HEIGHT: 18 to 24 inches

SPREAD: 15 inches

DESCRIPTION: Fuzzy, gray-green, triangular leaves grow in pairs along branches. An abundance of branches forms a dense perennial mat that gives off a pungent scent when crushed. Cats enjoy lying and rolling on catnip because of its aroma.

EASE OF CARE: Easy

HOW TO GROW: Catnip grows well in full sun to partial shade in average to sandy, well-drained soil.

PROPAGATION: By seed in spring or fall; by cuttings of active growth in early summer.

USES: *Fresh leaves*—candied

Dried leaves—teas, cat toys

PRESERVATION: Gather them in late summer just before they are in full bloom. Hang-dry the plants, remove leaves from stems, and store them in airtight containers.

Chamomile

PERENNIAL

BOTANICAL NAME: *Chamaemelum nobile*

HEIGHT: 9 to 12 inches

SPREAD: 4 to 6 inches

DESCRIPTION: These fine-leaved plants look almost like ferns, but they have a very strong aromatic scent. Over time, perennial chamomile will spread by means of underground shoots to form a solid mat that, if desired, can be kept mowed about 3 inches high. It produces an abundance of small daisylike flowers.

EASE OF CARE: Easy

HOW TO GROW: Chamomile grows in full sun in average to poor soils that are light and dry. Plant them in a group for impact.

PROPAGATION: By seed in early spring; by division in spring or fall.

USES: *Dried flowers*—teas, lotions
Dried plants—hair rinses, baths, potpourris

PRESERVATION: Harvest whole plants or flowers when petals begin to turn back onto the center. Hang-dry plants; screen-dry flowers.

OTHER VARIETIES: German chamomile (*Matricaria recutita*) is very similar and is used in the same ways as the perennial chamomile. However, since it's an annual, it must be grown from seed each spring. It grows to 24 inches and cannot be mowed.

Chervil

ANNUAL

BOTANICAL NAME: *Anthriscus cerefolium*

HEIGHT: 18 inches

SPREAD: 4 to 8 inches

DESCRIPTION: Lacy, fernlike, dark-green leaves have a coarser texture than carrot foliage, but finer than parsley. Chervil has a very delicate flavor of a licorice/parsley blend. Of the two forms available, the curly variety is more decorative in the garden than the flat variety.

EASE OF CARE: Average to difficult

HOW TO GROW: Chervil likes coolness and does well in partial shade. It likes a moist, well-drained, average or better soil. Do not try to move plants. For a fresh supply throughout the season, plant at 3-week intervals.

PROPAGATION: By seed in the fall or very early spring.

USES: *Fresh or frozen leaves*—eggs, salads, soups, fish, stews, veal. Add during the last few minutes of cooking.
Dried flowers—floral arrangements
Dried leaves—potpourri

PRESERVATION: Pick chervil just before blooming. For culinary use, freeze leaves or store them in a small amount of oil.

Chives

PERENNIAL

BOTANICAL NAME: *Allium schoenoprasum*

HEIGHT: 8 to 12 inches

SPREAD: 8 inches

DESCRIPTION: Chives have very tight clumps of long, skinny, grasslike leaves. They produce an abundance of small, rosy purple, globe-shaped flowers in early summer. Chives have a mild onion flavor.

EASE OF CARE: Easy

HOW TO GROW: This herb prefers an average to rich, moist soil, but will manage in almost any soil if kept moist. It grows in full sun to partial shade. It can also be grown as a potted plant indoors all year.

PROPAGATION: By seed or division taken during the growing season.

USES: *Fresh, dried, or frozen leaves*—cream cheese spreads, cottage cheese, potatoes, salads, eggs, soups, poultry, fish, shellfish, veal

Fresh flowers—vinegars, salads, garnishes

Dried flowers—floral arrangements, wreaths

PRESERVATION: Harvest only part of the plant at a time for continuous production through the season. Mince leaves and then freeze them for full flavor; dried leaves are less flavorful. Hang-dry the flowers for decorative uses. Pick them before any seeds begin to appear.

Coriander, Cilantro

ANNUAL

BOTANICAL NAME: *Coriandrum sativum*

HEIGHT: 24 to 36 inches

SPREAD: 6 inches

DESCRIPTION: Also known as Chinese Parsley, the lacy, bright-green leaves look very similar to flat-leaved Italian parsley on the lower part of the plant, but become more fernlike further up. This large annual has a leaf and root flavor that is a cross between sage and citrus; the seeds, however, are simply citruslike.

EASE OF CARE: Easy

HOW TO GROW: Plant in rich, well-drained soil in sun. Coriander plants are best located where they are protected from the wind, since they blow over easily.

PROPAGATION: By seed once the soil is warm in spring.

USES: *Fresh or frozen leaves*—salsa, potatoes, clams, oysters

Seeds—marinades, cheeses, pickles, mushrooms, stews, curries, chicken, quick breads, potpourris

Fresh roots—salads, relishes

PRESERVATION: Harvest only fresh, young leaves and freeze them promptly. Harvest seeds when they have turned brown, but are not yet released. Cut a whole plant and hang-dry inside paper bags to catch seeds.

Costmary

PERENNIAL

BOTANICAL NAME:
Chrysanthemum balsamita

HEIGHT: 30 to 36 inches

SPREAD: 24 inches

DESCRIPTION: Basal clusters of elongated oval leaves look similar to horseradish growth. This perennial sends up tall flower stems that produce clusters of unremarkable blooms. When the leaves are young and fresh, they're mint scented; the scent changes to balsam when the leaves are dried.

EASE OF CARE: Easy

HOW TO GROW: Grow in fertile, well-drained soil, in full sun to partial shade. Divide every few years as the clump becomes too large.

PROPAGATION: By division as needed.

USES: *Fresh leaves*—tuna fish, shrimp, eggs, lemonade

Dried leaves—sachets, potpourris, baths, lotions

PRESERVATION: Pick leaves when they are young and tender for immediate fresh use or a few at a time to dry. Costmary retains its scent for a long period when dried.

Dill

ANNUAL

BOTANICAL NAME: Anethum graveolens

HEIGHT: 24 to 36 inches

SPREAD: 6 inches

DESCRIPTION: Dill has extremely fine-cut, fernlike leaves on tall stems. It is a blue-green annual with attractive yellow flower umbels and yellow-green seed heads.

EASE OF CARE: Easy

HOW TO GROW: Dill likes acid, light, moist, and sandy soil in full sun. Since it does not transplant well, sow it in place and thin. Grow it in clumps or rows so stems can give support to one another.

PROPAGATION: By seed in late fall or early spring. Plant at 3-week intervals during spring and early summer for a fresh supply all season.

USES: *Fresh leaves*—potatoes, tomatoes, vinegars, pickles, fish, shrimp, stews, cheeses, lamb, pork, poultry

Fresh and dried seed heads—floral arrangements

Seeds—pickles, cheeses

PRESERVATION: Clip fresh leaves as needed. Flavor is best retained for winter use if frozen; pick the leaves just as flowers begin to open. For seeds, harvest entire plants when seed heads are brown but not yet releasing seeds. Hang-dry in paper bags to catch seeds.

Fennel

PERENNIAL

BOTANICAL NAME: *Foeniculum vulgare*

HEIGHT: 50 to 72 inches

SPREAD: 18 to 36 inches

DESCRIPTION: Fennel has very fine cut leaves that look similar to dill. This half-hardy perennial has a sweetish, licoricelike flavor.

EASE OF CARE: Easy

HOW TO GROW: Fennel likes alkaline soil; add lime if soil is very acid. Grow in full sun in well-drained, rich soil. Locate them where plants are sheltered from heavy winds since they blow over easily.

PROPAGATION: By seed in cold climates, where it will grow as an annual. Sow in late fall or early spring.

USES: *Fresh leaves*—sauces, salads, eggs, fish

Dried leaves—cosmetic oils, soaps, facials

Seeds—desserts, cakes, breads, potatoes, spreads

PRESERVATION: Snip individual leaves to use fresh or to freeze. Harvest whole plants just before blooming and hang-dry. To harvest seeds, cut down entire plants when seeds turn brown but before they release. Hang-dry in paper bags to catch the seeds.

OTHER VARIETIES: Sweet fennel, *Foeniculum vulgare dulce,* is a closely related annual, the base stems of which are eaten as a vegetable.

Garlic Chives

PERENNIAL

BOTANICAL NAME: *Allium tuberosum*

HEIGHT: 18 inches

SPREAD: 8 inches

DESCRIPTION: Garlic chives (also known as Chinese Chives and Chinese Leeks) have compact, grasslike clumps of large, flattened, blue-green leaves that look like a larger version of chives. This perennial has white globe-shaped blossoms that last a long time in floral arrangements. It has a definite garlic flavor.

EASE OF CARE: Easy

HOW TO GROW: Plant seeds in full sun in average to poor soil.

PROPAGATION: By seed in spring; by division anytime during the growing season.

USES: *Fresh leaves*—salads, soups, spreads, vinegars

Dried leaves—soups, cheeses, sauces

Fresh and dried flowers—floral arrangements

PRESERVATION: Harvest only part of the plant at a time for continuous production throughout the season. Mince leaves and then freeze them for full flavor; drying causes some flavor loss. Hang-dry flowers for decorative uses.

Geraniums, scented

HALF-HARDY PERENNIAL

BOTANICAL NAME: *Pelargonium* species

HEIGHT: Varies with variety

SPREAD: Varies with variety

DESCRIPTION: These aromatic-leaved perennials come in a variety of scents. The leaf shapes are also varied, ranging from round to deeply cut, and their color ranges from yellow-green to reddish-purple according to the variety involved.

EASE OF CARE: Average

HOW TO GROW: All prefer full sun and well-drained, rich to average soil. Geraniums overwinter as potted plants in cold climates.

PROPAGATION: By cuttings before flowering.

USES: *Fresh leaves*—cakes, cookies, jellies

Dried leaves—potpourris, sachets, baths, facials, teas

Fresh flowers—salads

PRESERVATION: Pick single leaves just as plants begin to develop flower buds and dry them on screens.

VARIETIES: Lemon geranium is *P. mellissinum,* lime is *P. nervosum,* apple is *P. odoratissimum,* and peppermint is *P. tomentosum.* These are probably the most common of the many special scented geranium varieties available.

Horehound

PERENNIAL

BOTANICAL NAME: *Marrubium vulgare*

HEIGHT: 30 inches

SPREAD: 12 inches

DESCRIPTION: Horehound has round, gray, mintlike foliage. The overall look of this perennial is that of a woolly, gray bush. It makes an attractive addition to any garden. Flower arrangers will find it an outstanding decorative foliage for fresh or dried use.

EASE OF CARE: Easy

HOW TO GROW: Grow in full sun in average to poor, well-drained soil.

PROPAGATION: By seed or division in late spring.

USES: *Fresh or dried leaves*—candy flavorings, teas

Dried branches—floral arrangements

PRESERVATION: Remove the leaves from the stems at the time of flowering and dry them on screens. Store in airtight containers. Hang-dry whole branches.

Horseradish

PERENNIAL

BOTANICAL NAME: *Armoracia rusticana*

HEIGHT: 36 to 60 inches

SPREAD: 18 to 24 inches

DESCRIPTION: Horseradish is a perennial with a deep, spreading root topped with a cluster of large, coarse, yellow-green leaves. The root has a very sharp, radishlike flavor.

EASE OF CARE: Easy

HOW TO GROW: Plant in full sun to partial shade, in well-drained soil.

PROPAGATION: By seed or division in the spring; by root cuttings in early summer.

USES: *Fresh leaves*—baths

Roots—ground with white vinegar or mayonnaise to accompany fish, beef, potato salads, beets

PRESERVATION: Harvest roots in late fall and store in root cellar or similar winter storage area for root crops. When ready to use, peel, grind, put into a glass jar, cover, and mix with white vinegar; store in refrigerator.

Hyssop

PERENNIAL

BOTANICAL NAME: *Hyssopus officinalis*

HEIGHT: 18 inches

SPREAD: 12 inches

DESCRIPTION: This neat, low, shrubby plant has leaves growing in whorls around stiff, upright stems. It makes a good edging plant and can be clipped in order to keep its shape. This attractive perennial has a mint-like, but bitter flavor.

EASE OF CARE: Average

HOW TO GROW: Prefers full sun, but can tolerate partial shade. Plant it in well-drained soil that is high in lime. Cut hyssop back each spring to encourage new growth.

PROPAGATION: By division in the spring; by seed in late summer for early spring; by cuttings taken in early summer; or by layering.

USES: *Fresh leaves*—salads, soups, fruit salads, lamb, poultry, teas

Dried leaves—teas, perfumes, potpourris, baths, facials

PRESERVATION: Harvest hyssop just as it's about to flower. Hang-dry and use it whole for facials and baths, or remove leaves from stems for use in tea or potpourri.

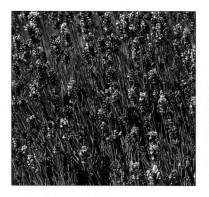 

Lavender

PERENNIAL

BOTANICAL NAME: *Lavandula angustifolia*

HEIGHT: 36 to 48 inches

SPREAD: 18 to 30 inches

DESCRIPTION: Lavender has silver-gray, needlelike foliage on a bushy, spreading plant. This perennial produces individual flower stalks topped by attractive purple-blue, pink, or white clusters of bloom.

EASE OF CARE: Average

HOW TO GROW: Grow in full sun in well-drained, sandy, alkaline soil.

PROPAGATION: By cuttings before flowering or by layering.

USES: *Fresh leaves*—vinegar, jellies
Dried leaves—facials, baths
Fresh flowers—candy, vinegars, floral arrangements
Dried flowers—potpourris, sachets, perfumes, soaps, bath powders, wreaths, floral arrangements
Dried branches—baths, wreaths, floral arrangements

PRESERVATION: Pick separate leaves and 3- to 4-inch active growth tips in spring and summer. Dry on screens. Harvest flowers when they are in the late bud stage, just before they actually bloom. Hang-dry.

OTHER VARIETIES: There are a number of different species and cultivars of lavender available. The differences between them focus primarily on flower color, size, and growth habit.

Lavender-Cotton

PERENNIAL

BOTANICAL NAME: *Santolina chamaecyparissus*

HEIGHT: 12 to 18 inches

SPREAD: 18 inches

DESCRIPTION: Very light silver-gray, cottony evergreen foliage produces an interesting knobby look. Also known as Santolina, these spreading plants are very dense. They're great as edgings or clipped into low hedges. Each flower grows on a separate stem.

EASE OF CARE: Easy

HOW TO GROW: Lavender-cotton likes full sun and poor, sandy, preferably alkaline soil. It can be cut back each spring to encourage new growth. In very cold climates, either provide winter protection or grow plants in pots and bring them indoors for the cold season.

PROPAGATION: By seed in spring, propagation by cuttings in early summer, or division by layering.

USES: *Dried leaves*—potpourris, sachets
Dried flowers—wreaths, floral arrangements
Fresh branches—floral arrangements
Dried branches—floral arrangements, baths

PRESERVATION: Harvest foliage in late summer; flowers should be harvested just as they start to come into bloom. Hang-dry.

Lemon Balm

PERENNIAL

BOTANICAL NAME: *Melissa officinalis*

HEIGHT: 48 inches

SPREAD: 18 inches

DESCRIPTION: A full, attractive perennial with shield-shaped leaves, lemon balm spreads readily by seed. As its name suggests, it smells of lemon.

EASE OF CARE: Easy

HOW TO GROW: Lemon balm prospers in full sun, but will also do well in partial shade. It likes a well-drained or moist, sandy soil. It grows abundantly.

PROPAGATION: By seed in the autumn or early spring; by cuttings in the spring and summer; by division in spring or fall.

USES: *Fresh leaves*—salads, cold beverages, jellies

Dried leaves—potpourris, perfumes

PRESERVATION: Pick in midsummer and hang-dry branches or spread single leaves on screening to dry.

OTHER VARIETIES: Bee balm, *Monarda didyma,* is not a related species, but is similar in its growth, propagation, and uses. It prefers moist, average to fertile soil for best growth.

Lovage

PERENNIAL

BOTANICAL NAME: *Levisticum officinalis*

HEIGHT: 60 inches

SPREAD: 30 inches

DESCRIPTION: Lovage is a large, handsome perennial plant with glossy, dark green, cut-leaf foliage. The flavor is like that of celery, but somewhat sweeter and stronger.

EASE OF CARE: Average

HOW TO GROW: Lovage likes moist, rich, acid soil. It will grow in full sun or partial shade. Since it dies down completely during the winter, mark its place in the fall to avoid damage.

PROPAGATION: By seed in late summer; by division in autumn or early spring.

USES: *Fresh, frozen, or dried leaves*—stews, soups

Fresh leaves—salads

Fresh stems—salads, soups, steamed vegetables

Seeds—pickles, cheeses, salads, dressings, potatoes, tomatoes, chicken

PRESERVATION: Use fresh as needed. Pick for winter use just before the plant begins to bloom. To freeze, blanch small amounts at a time, quick cool, and freeze as is, or chop and freeze in cubes. Alternatively, hang-dry. For seeds, pick seed heads when they turn brown but before they release. Hang-dry inside paper bags to catch seeds.

Marjoram

PERENNIAL, often grown as Annual

BOTANICAL NAME: *Origanum majorana* or *Majorana hortensis*

HEIGHT: 8 to 12 inches

SPREAD: 12 to 18 inches

DESCRIPTION: Marjoram is a bushy, spreading, half-hardy perennial that is grown as an annual in climates where it freezes. It has small, oval, gray-green, velvety leaves. This plant is attractive when grown as a potted plant and brought indoors to overwinter.

EASE OF CARE: Easy

HOW TO GROW: Marjoram likes rich, well-drained alkaline soil and full sun. Where winters are severe, treat it as an annual or as a potted plant. Locate it in a sheltered spot for best overwinter survival outdoors.

PROPAGATION: By seed early indoors, transplanting seedlings outdoors after danger of frost has passed; by cuttings in spring.

USES: *Fresh or dried leaves*—stuffings, soups, stews, meat loaf, pork, poultry, fish, eggs, potatoes, cheeses. Can be used in place of oregano.

Dried leaves—baths, potpourris, sachets

Dried flowers—floral arrangements, wreaths

PRESERVATION: Snip fresh when needed. For drying, harvest just before flowering and hang-dry.

Nasturtium

ANNUAL

BOTANICAL NAME: *Tropaeolum majus*

HEIGHT: 12 inches for bush, 72 inches for vines

SPREAD: 18 inches for bush

DESCRIPTION: Distinctive, blue-green circular leaves are held up on fleshy stems. These annuals come in a variety of types ranging from compact bushes to long-spreading vines. They make an eye-catching addition to any garden. In addition, they have large attractive blooms that range in color from pale yellows, pinks, and apricots to deep, rich yellows, oranges, and burgundy. The vining types are great in hanging planters, window boxes, or for use on trellises and fences. Aphids love nasturtiums, so be on the lookout for them.

EASE OF CARE: Easy

HOW TO GROW: Plant in full sun to partial shade in average to poor, moist soil.

PROPAGATION: By seed in late spring. They're large and can be planted individually where the plants are going to grow.

USES: *Fresh leaves and flowers*—salads

Fresh flowers—floral arrangements

Unripe seeds and flower buds—pickled for salads

PRESERVATION: Pickle unripe seeds in vinegar and use them in salads.

Oregano

PERENNIAL

BOTANICAL NAME: *Origanum vulgare*

HEIGHT: 18 inches

SPREAD: 12 inches

DESCRIPTION: Oregano is a bushy, spreading perennial with abundant oval leaves and purple blooms. Be careful to get the correct species. To be sure of avoiding disappointment, buy a plant that you've tested by crushing a few leaves and smelling or tasting them beforehand. It should have the distinct aroma of oregano.

EASE OF CARE: Easy

HOW TO GROW: Grow in full sun, in average to sandy and preferably alkaline soil (add lime generously if soil is acid).

PROPAGATION: Buy your first plant, then obtain additional ones by division, layering, or cuttings.

USES: *Fresh or dried leaves*—tomatoes, cheeses, eggs, beef, pork, poultry, shellfish, potatoes, sauces

Flowers—floral arrangements

Dried branches—baths

PRESERVATION: Clip fresh as needed. Harvest at the time of bloom and hang-dry or freeze.

Parsley

BIENNIAL

BOTANICAL NAME: *Petroselinum crispum*

HEIGHT: 12 inches

SPREAD: 8 inches

DESCRIPTION: Attractive, dense, rich-green leaves form a rosette base. A biennial usually grown as an annual, parsley comes in two cut-leaf forms: ruffled and Italian. The latter has flat leaves and is stronger-flavored than the ruffled variety. The ruffled form makes a nice edging plant; both are also easily grown as indoor potted plants.

EASE OF CARE: Easy

HOW TO GROW: Plant in place in full sun or partial shade in moist, rich soil. Presoak seeds several hours in warm water to help speed up germination.

PROPAGATION: By seed once the soil is warm.

USES: *Fresh, dried, or frozen leaves*—garnishes, potatoes, soups, sauces, pasta, poultry, jellies, baths, shampoos, lotions

PRESERVATION: Snip as needed fresh. Hang-dry the flat variety; snip and freeze the ruffled variety.

Peppermint

PERENNIAL

BOTANICAL NAME: Mentha piperita

HEIGHT: 24 to 30 inches

SPREAD: 12 inches

DESCRIPTION: Peppermint has dark-green, spear-shaped leaves that come to a point. It has a neat, dense growth habit with tall stems arising from an underground network of spreading stems. Since it can become invasive, plant it in an isolated location or where it can be kept contained. Another alternative is to grow it as a potted plant.

EASE OF CARE: Easy

HOW TO GROW: Likes full sun or partial shade and rich, moist soil.

PROPAGATION: By cuttings taken in mid-summer; by division at any time during the growing season.

USES: Fresh or frozen leaves—garnishes, vinegars, jellies, punches, candy, lamb

Dried leaves—teas

PRESERVATION: Pick shoots in early to mid-summer. Hang-dry or freeze.

OTHER VARIETIES: Pineapple mint, apple mint, and lemon mint each have flavors as indicated by their names. (Also refer to the profile on Spearmint.)

Rosemary

PERENNIAL

BOTANICAL NAME: Rosmarinus officinalis

HEIGHT: 48 to 72 inches

SPREAD: 18 to 24 inches

DESCRIPTION: Rosemary is an attractive, evergreen perennial with a spreading habit of growth. Its gray-green, needle-shaped foliage can be pruned to form a low hedge. Grow rosemary as a potted plant in colder climates to protect it from winter winds. It makes an attractive addition to any garden. There is a prostrate form that makes a wonderful ground cover where hardy.

EASE OF CARE: Average

HOW TO GROW: Likes a sandy, alkaline soil and full sun.

PROPAGATION: By cuttings or by seed in spring, or by layering.

USES: Fresh or frozen leaves—fish, lamb, potatoes, soups, tomatoes, pork, poultry, cheeses, eggs, breads, fruit salads, jellies

Dried leaves—facials, hair rinses, sachets, potpourris, lotions, toilet waters

Fresh and dried branches—baths

PRESERVATION: Pick rosemary fresh as desired. Hang-dry or freeze the active, young 3- to 4-inch growth tips.

Rue

PERENNIAL

BOTANICAL NAME: *Ruta graveolens*

HEIGHT: 24 inches

SPREAD: 18 inches

DESCRIPTION: This perennial has blue-green, teardrop-shaped foliage in clusters. Rue is an attractive and unusual plant to use as a focal point in a garden design.

EASE OF CARE: Average

HOW TO GROW: Full sun in poor, sandy, alkaline soil. It can also be easily grown as a pot plant.

PROPAGATION: By seed in spring or started ahead of time indoors and transplanted into the garden after the danger of frost has passed; by cuttings in mid-summer.

USES: *Fresh leaves*—floral arrangements, tussy mussies

Dried seed heads—floral arrangements

PRESERVATION: Pick just before flowers open and hang-dry. Collect seeds when flower heads ripen.

OTHER VARIETIES: "Jackman's Blue" is compact with very blue leaves. It can also be trimmed to form a lovely low hedge.

Sage

PERENNIAL

BOTANICAL NAME: *Salvia officinalis*

HEIGHT: 20 inches

SPREAD: 24 inches

DESCRIPTION: Sage is a perennial with gray-green, pebblelike, textured leaves in a long, oval shape. It has an attractive, compact, spreading growth habit. This plant is also available in variegated and purple-leaved varieties. Sage is a good edging plant and is attractive in any garden.

EASE OF CARE: Easy

HOW TO GROW: Grow it in full sun in a well-drained, sandy, alkaline soil. Protect it from the wind.

PROPAGATION: By seed, cuttings, or division by layering in the spring.

USES: *Fresh, frozen, or dried leaves*—salads, breads, soups, stews, pork, beef, fish, lamb, poultry, stuffings, tomatoes, vegetables, cheeses, teas

Dried branches—baths, lotions, herb wreaths

PRESERVATION: Use fresh sage as needed. Pick active growth shoots or separate leaves to hang-dry, screen-dry, or freeze.

OTHER VARIETIES: Sage is available in gold and green variegated (*S. officinalis 'Aurea'*) and purple-leaved (*S. officinalis 'Purpurea'*) varieties.

Savory, Summer

ANNUAL

BOTANICAL NAME: *Satureja hortensis*

HEIGHT: 18 inches

SPREAD: 8 inches

DESCRIPTION: This attractive annual has flattened, gray-green, needle-shaped leaves. The leaves are soft rather than stiff and have a slightly peppery flavor. The overall look of the plant is light and airy.

EASE OF CARE: Easy

HOW TO GROW: Plant seeds in place in full sun in a light, rich to average soil. They do not transplant well. Summer savory grows well as a container plant with seeds planted directly in a pot.

PROPAGATION: By seed when the soil is warm.

USES: *Fresh, dried, or frozen leaves*—tomatoes, pastas, soups, stews, roasts, beans, salads, cheeses, fish, vinegars, vegetables

PRESERVATION: When it begins to flower, dry on screens or paper.

Sorrel, French

PERENNIAL

BOTANICAL NAME: *Rumex acetosa* or *R. scutatus*

HEIGHT: 18 inches

SPREAD: 10 inches

DESCRIPTION: Succulent, bright green, spear-shaped leaves in a low rosette send up tall flower stalks that should be removed so that leaf supply will continue. The leaves of this hardy perennial have a pleasant acidity that brightens any salad. Sorrel can also be grown as an indoor potted plant.

EASE OF CARE: Easy

HOW TO GROW: Provide full sun or partial shade in a moist, rich acid soil. Shady conditions produce a milder taste.

PROPAGATION: By seed or division in spring.

USES: *Fresh or frozen leaves*—soups, lamb, beef, sauces

PRESERVATION: Remove single leaves and use them fresh or freeze them for winter use.

Southernwood

PERENNIAL

BOTANICAL NAME: *Artemisia abrotanum*

HEIGHT: 30 inches

SPREAD: 24 inches

DESCRIPTION: Woolly, silver-gray, cut leaves and a dense, branching growth habit make these perennials a very decorative addition to any garden.

EASE OF CARE: Easy

HOW TO GROW: Full sun in any kind of soil. Prune southernwood back each spring to encourage new growth and a nice shape.

PROPAGATION: By semi-hardwood cuttings in late summer.

USES: *Fresh branches*—floral arrangements, tussy mussies

Dried branches—baths, floral arrangements, wreaths

PRESERVATION: Pick branches just before flowering and hang-dry.

Spearmint

PERENNIAL

BOTANICAL NAME: *Mentha spicata* or *M. viridis*

HEIGHT: 20 inches

SPREAD: 12 inches

DESCRIPTION: Green, pointed leaves are somewhat hairy compared to peppermint, but the best way to tell them apart is to crush the leaves and taste or smell them. Spearmint has a neat, dense growth with tall stems rising from a network of spreading underground stems. It can become invasive, so plant it in an isolated location or where it can be kept contained. A good solution is to grow it as a potted plant.

EASE OF CARE: Easy

HOW TO GROW: Full sun or partial shade in rich, moist soil.

PROPAGATION: By cuttings in mid-summer; by division at any time during the growing season.

USES: *Fresh or frozen leaves*—candy, garnishes, jellies, punches, lamb

Dried leaves—teas

PRESERVATION: Pick shoots in early to mid-summer. Hang-dry or freeze.

OTHER VARIETIES: Pineapple mint, apple mint, and lemon mint each have distinctive flavors as indicated by their name. (Also refer to the profile on Peppermint.)

Sweet Woodruff

PERENNIAL

BOTANICAL NAME: *Galium odoratum* or *Asperula odorata*

HEIGHT: 6 to 8 inches

SPREAD: 6 to 8 inches

DESCRIPTION: Single, small, knife-shaped leaves circle in tiers around the stemlike flattened wheel spokes. This perennial has a rich green color and spreads by means of underground stems to make a lovely ground cover when it has its preferred growing conditions of shade and rich, moist soil.

EASE OF CARE: Difficult unless conditions are exactly to its liking.

HOW TO GROW: Grow in rich, moist soil in fairly deep woodland shade.

PROPAGATION: By seed in fall that will sprout in the spring; by division after flowering.

USES: *Fresh leaves*—wine punches
Dried leaves—potpourris, sachets, wreaths

PRESERVATION: Pick fresh sweet woodruff as needed. Cut entire stems when in bloom and hang-dry.

Tansy

PERENNIAL

BOTANICAL NAME: *Tanacetum vulgare*

HEIGHT: 40 inches

SPREAD: 12 to 18 inches

DESCRIPTION: This hardy perennial has lush, dark-green, cut leaves and tall flower stems that produce tight clusters of intense yellow, button-shaped blooms. These are vigorous growers that spread rapidly and can take over; keep them constantly under control or place them where they can run wild. The foliage has a strong peppery odor and flavor.

EASE OF CARE: Easy

HOW TO GROW: Grow in full sun or partial shade in average to poor soil.

PROPAGATION: By seed in spring; by division in spring or fall; or by layering.

USES: *Fresh or dried flowers*—floral arrangements

PRESERVATION: Harvest leaves singly and dry them on screens or harvest entire stems with flowers and hang-dry.

Tarragon

PERENNIAL

BOTANICAL NAME: *Artemisia dracunculus*

HEIGHT: 24 inches

SPREAD: 24 inches

DESCRIPTION: This bushy, medium-green perennial has pointed leaves and inconspicuous flowers. Be sure to get the French rather than the Russian variety that looks very much the same with somewhat narrower and lighter green leaves. However, the latter has none of the sweetly aromatic flavor wanted for culinary use.

EASE OF CARE: Average

HOW TO GROW: Likes full sun to partial shade in a sandy to rich alkaline soil that is well drained. Cut it back in the fall or early spring. Protect it with a mulch during the winter in cold climates.

PROPAGATION: Buy your first plant, then by cuttings in summer and fall; by division in early spring; or by layering.

USES: *Fresh, dried, or frozen leaves*—fish, vinegars, tomatoes, salads, eggs, chicken, pickles

PRESERVATION: Pick separate leaves any time for fresh use. Pick just before blooming to freeze or dry. Store immediately in an airtight container. The flavor can also be captured in vinegar or oil.

Thyme

PERENNIAL

BOTANICAL NAME: *Thymus vulgaris*

HEIGHT: 1 to 10 inches depending on variety

SPREAD: 12 to 18 inches

DESCRIPTION: These wide-spreading perennials make a good and inexpensive ground cover. Their profuse blooms are especially attractive to bees; clip off flower heads just before blooming.

EASE OF CARE: Easy

HOW TO GROW: Thyme does well in full sun to partial shade in poor to average, well-drained soil. Trim it back each spring to encourage abundant new growth.

PROPAGATION: By seed or division in spring or fall; by cuttings in early summer; or by layering.

USES: *Fresh, frozen, or dried leaves*—marinades, stuffings, soups, vinegars, poultry, shellfish, fish, cheeses

Dried leaves—sachets, potpourris, floral arrangements, baths, facials, wreaths

Dried flowers—sachets, lotions, baths

PRESERVATION: Harvest anytime for fresh use. Pick before and during flowering to hang-dry.

OTHER VARIETIES: There are many different thyme species and varieties with self-descriptive names, all good candidates for use in garden design.

Wormwood

PERENNIAL

BOTANICAL NAME: *Artemisia absinthium*

HEIGHT: 30 to 48 inches

SPREAD: 15 to 20 inches

DESCRIPTION: A handsome, very fine, cut-leaf, silver-green foliage and a spreading growth habit make this an attractive perennial.

EASE OF CARE: Average

HOW TO GROW: Plant in full sun in almost any kind of soil as long as it's alkaline. Add lime if soil is naturally acid.

PROPAGATION: By seed or cuttings in summer; by division in spring or fall.

USES: *Fresh leaves*—floral arrangements

Dried leaves—sachets, floral arrangements, wreaths

PRESERVATION: Harvest when in flower and hang-dry.